TODD AND CRAIG'S
Perhapanauts™

THE PERHAPANAUTS CREATED BY TODD DEZAGO & CRAIG ROUSSEAU

TODD AND CRAIG'S
THE Perhapanauts

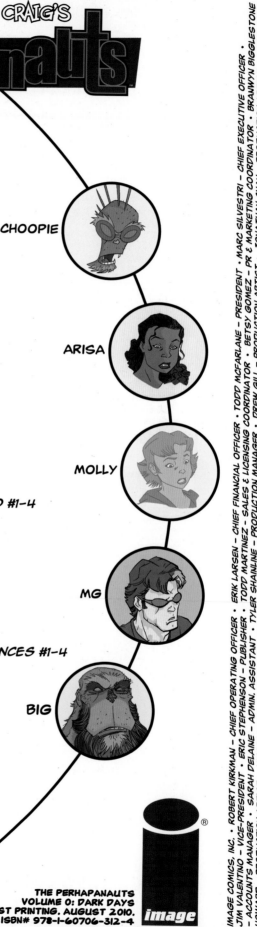

CHOOPIE

ARISA

MOLLY

MG

BIG

THERE ARE PLACES IN THIS WORLD WHERE THE FABRIC OF REALITY HAS WORN THIN, WHERE STRANGE AND TERRIBLE CREATURES HAVE CROSSED OVER TO LURK IN THE SHADOWS AND THE NIGHT.

THERE IS AN ORGANIZATION DEDICATED TO FINDING THESE CREATURES AND SENDING THEM BACK WHENCE THEY CAME, SEALING THE RIFT BEHIND THEM, AND MAINTAINING THE INTEGRITY OF THOSE BORDERS.

THE ORGANIZATION IS CALLED BEDLAM. ITS AGENTS ARE...
THE PERHAPANAUTS

IMAGE COMICS, INC. • ROBERT KIRKMAN – CHIEF OPERATING OFFICER • ERIK LARSEN – CHIEF FINANCIAL OFFICER • TODD MCFARLANE – PRESIDENT • MARC SILVESTRI – CHIEF EXECUTIVE OFFICER • JIM VALENTINO – VICE-PRESIDENT • ERIC STEPHENSON – PUBLISHER • TODD MARTINEZ – SALES & LICENSING COORDINATOR • BETSY GOMEZ – PR & MARKETING COORDINATOR • BRANWYN BIGGLESTONE – ACCOUNTS MANAGER • SARAH DELAINE – ADMIN. ASSISTANT • TYLER SHAINLINE – PRODUCTION MANAGER • DREW GILL – PRODUCTION ARTIST • JONATHAN CHAN – PRODUCTION ARTIST • MONICA HOWARD – PRODUCTION ARTIST • VINCENT KUKUA – PRODUCTION ARTIST • KEVIN YUEN – PRODUCTION ARTIST • WWW.IMAGECOMICS.COM

THE PERHAPANAUTS
VOLUME 0: DARK DAYS
FIRST PRINTING. AUGUST 2010.
ISBN# 978-1-60706-312-4

image®

• INTRODUCTION •

"FOR AS LONG AS I CAN REMEMBER."

THAT'S WHAT I TELL PEOPLE WHEN THEY ASK HOW LONG I'VE HAD AN INTEREST IN THE PARANORMAL. INTEREST. FASCINATION. AND, AT TIMES, YES, OBSESSION.

I DIDN'T LIKE MONSTERS AS A KID. I DIDN'T LIKE BEING FRIGHTENED. IT WASN'T UNTIL I WAS IN MY 'TEENS THAT I LEARNED TO LOVE TO BE SCARED, AND EVEN THEN IT WASN'T THE MOVIE MONSTERS, YOUR FRANKENSTEINS, DRACULAS, OR WEREWOLVES, THAT PIQUED MY CURIOSITY-- THOUGH I CERTAINLY KNEW WHO THEY WERE. IT WAS THE 'REAL' MONSTERS THAT LURKED IN THE NIGHT, THAT INHABITED THE VAST, SPARSELY-EXPLORED WILDERNESS, THE LAKES AND THE FORESTS, POSSIBLY NO FARTHER THAN YOUR OWN BACKYARD.

BIGFOOT.

THE LOCH NESS MONSTER.

GHOSTS. ALIENS. UFOS.

AND LATER, MOTHMAN, EL CHUPACABRAS, AND THE DOVER DEMON.

AND SO IT WAS, ALL THOSE YEARS AGO, WHEN CRAIG AND I FIRST BECAME FRIENDS AND DECIDED TO COLLABORATE ON "SOME FUN, SMALL PROJECT", THAT HE SUGGESTED THAT I "WRITE WHAT I KNOW"...AND THE PERHAPANAUTS WERE BORN. SOON CRAIG AND I FOUND OURSELVES TO BE THE PROUD PARENTS OF A FAMILY CONSISTING OF SEVERAL BIZARRE CREATURES, A FEW INDIVIDUALS WITH SOME RATHER UNIQUE ABILITIES, AND A CUTE LITTLE TEENAGE GHOST. WITH MY EXHAUSTIVE KNOWLEDGE OF THINGS UNKNOWN AND UNEXPLAINED, I FELT, I COULD HAVE THEM INVESTIGATE A NEW CRYPTID OR ANOMALOUS EVENT EVERY ISSUE AND NEVER RUN OUT OF FODDER FOR STORIES.

THAT WAS THE PLAN ANYWAY.

BUT SOON THE CHARACTERS DEVELOPED VOICES OF THEIR OWN AND THEIR ADVENTURES BEGAN EXPANDING AND GOING IN DIRECTIONS CRAIG AND I HAD NEVER DISCUSSED, NEVER INTENDED. THE TEAM TOOK ON A LIFE OF THEIR OWN AND WE SOON REALIZED THAT WE WERE IN THE SERVICE OF THEIR DESTINIES AND NOT THE OTHER WAY AROUND.

THERE ARE MANY MORE ADVENTURES TO TELL AND, GOD WILLING, CRAIG AND I WILL CONTINUE TO CHURN THEM OUT WHEN WE CAN. BUT UNTIL THEN, WE PROUDLY PRESENT HERE, FOR THE FIRST TIME IN ONE VOLUME, THE EARLY ADVENTURES OF OUR 'HAPS, SO THAT YOU CAN SEE WHERE THEY CAME FROM. AND, IF YOU LOOK CLOSELY ENOUGH, WHERE THEY'RE GOING...

I'M A TEASE, RIGHT?

THESE TALES WERE ORIGINALLY PUBLISHED UNDER THE DARK HORSE BANNER AND CRAIG AND I WOULD LIKE TO THANK DAVE LAND AND KATIE MOODY FOR DOING A WONDERFUL JOB OF FERRYING THE BOOK TO PUBLICATION IN ITS TWO INCARNATIONS THERE. DAVE WAS A FUN, CREATIVE, AND ATTENTIVE EDITOR AND HE HAS OUR UNDYING GRATITUDE.

THAT'S IT. HERE'S OUR BOOK! JUMP IN AND ENJOY THE EARLY DAYS WITH BIG AND CHOOPIE, ARISA AND MOLLY, MG AND HAMMERSKOLD, AND, OF COURSE, KARL. OUR FAMILY.
AND NOW, YOU'RE PART OF THE FAMILY TOO...

SMELL YA LATER~!
TODD
ELIZAVILLE, NY
AUGUST 2010

DEDICATED TO MIKE AND JAKE

CHAPTER ON

c!

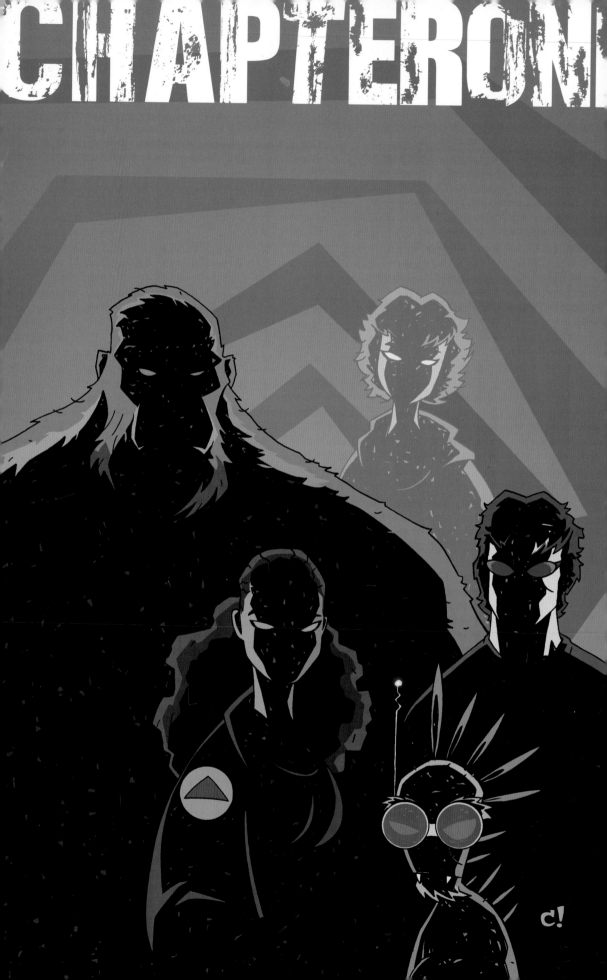

CANTELE
SELF STORAGE
sssh
UNITS AVAILABLE
Call 1-800-CAN-TELE

BEDLAM
BUREAU OF EXTRA-DIMENSIONAL LIABILITIES AND MANAGEMENT
BUREAU OF EXTRA-DIMENSIONAL LIABILITIES AND MANAGEMENT
ONEERING
BOTASH

ELDRITCH
COMSEC
CRYPTID
TODD AND CRAIG'S
THE Perhapanauts
"In Medias Res"
words-todd pictures-craig
colors-rico with whitney

HEY. HOW YA DOIN'?
NEW HERE, RIGHT?
WELL, THEN, WELCOME TO BEDLAM-- THE BUREAU OF EXTRA-DIMENSIONAL LIABILITIES AND MANAGEMENT.
I'M GUY. I GUESS I'M THE ONE'S S'POSE TO GIVE YOU THE 411 ON THE PLACE.
FIRST THING; DON'T GET LOST. I MEAN, THEY CAN FINDJA 'CAUSE THEY GOT THESE LITTLE LOCATOR CHIP-THINGIES BUILT INTA YER ID PASS. BUT THIS PLACE IS HUGE!...
...AND THERE'S SOME PARTS'AT CAN BE KINDA DANGEROUS...
GUY
BEDLAM
PLUS, IF THEY GOTTA COME LOOKIN' FOR YA, THEY BUST YA PRETTY HARD ABOUT IT AFTER.
HEH.
SO...
...YER WONDERIN' WHAT THEY DO HERE, RIGHT?

WELL, I'M NO *EXPERT* OR NOTHIN', BUT IF IT'S *SPOOKY*, THESE'RE THE GUYS THAT'RE CHECKIN' IT OUT. AN' THE *PARANORMALIER*, THE BETTER!
THEY'RE DOIN' *FREAKY* STUFF, LIKE SEANCES AND ESP AND MENTAL STUFF LIKE THAT...
BUT MOSTLY IT'S ABOUT THE *UNEXPLAINED*, THE *UNKNOWN* ...*CREEPY* STUFF.
NIGHTMARE STUFF.
LIKE THAT SOMETHIN' THAT YOU SEE OUTTA THE CORNER OF YER *EYE*, BUT WHEN YOU LOOK BACK, NOTHIN'S THERE.
OR WHEN YER SURE YA HEARD SOMEONE ***TALKIN'*** UPSTAIRS, BUT YOU KNOW YER THE ONLY ONE IN THE HOUSE.
OR THAT FEELIN' YA GET THAT YA ***KNOW*** SOMETHING'S WATCHIN' YOU FROM THE CORNER'A YER ROOM WHEN YOU WAKE UP IN THE ***DARK*** IN THE MIDDLE 'A THE NIGHT.

SEE, THE IDEA IS THAT THERE'S PLACES IN THIS WORLD WHERE THE FABRIC'A REALITY'S WORN THIN. AN' THERE'S LOTSA DIFFERENT DIMENSIONS OUT THERE--REALMS THEY CALL 'EM. AN' THEY'RE RIGHT HERE, RIGHT NEXTA OURS, BUT WE CAN'T SEE 'EM!
BIZARRE PLACES. PLACES JUST SO ...ALIEN T'WHAT WE KNOW...
AN' SOMETIMES THESE...THINGS...BREAK THROUGH AND SLIP INTA OUR WORLD. WHERE THEY SHOULDN'T BE. STRANGE, WEIRD CREATURES. AND USUALLY DANGEROUS.
SO BEDLAM'S GOT THESE TEAMS'A AGENTS--COUPLE OF 'EM--AND THESE GUYS'RE S'POSE TA PUSH 'EM BACK TO WHERE THEY CAME FROM AN' SEAL UP THE RIP.
AN' THEY DO! THEY'RE GOOD AT IT!
USUALLY...
WEIRD CREATURES.
BUT SEE, THE REALLY WEIRD THING IS THAT THE TEAMS...WELL, THE AGENTS... THE GUYS ON THE TEAMS ARE ACTUALLY...
WELL, WAIT. WHY DON' I JUST TELL YA ABOUT THE OTHER NIGHT.
'CAUSE IT'S LIKE IT ALWAYS HAPPENS AT NIGHT...

"NOW THESE RIFTS IN THE DIMENSIONAL BOUNDARIES I WAS TELLIN' YA ABOUT, THEY CAN'T BE DETECTED BY MACHINES'R NOTHIN', SO THE BEDLAM GUYS GET THAT INFORMATION A DIFFERENT WAY..."
41 DEGREES, 54 NORTH LATITUDE, 71 DEGREES, 7 WEST LONGITUDE.
AND... THE ...BUTTERFLIES TOLD HIM THAT?
YUP.
SIR, LEPID-V REPORTS A DISTURBANCE AT--
I HEARD, MARTIN. THANK YOU.
SCRAMBLE BLUE TEAM.
WOOT-WOOT-WOOT-WOOT-WOOT-WOOT-WOOT
"SEE, THE THING IS, WHAT I WAS TRYIN'A TELL YA BEFORE IS... THE AGENTS...
"...THEY'RE... REALLY WEIRD CREATURES THEMSELVES."

WHAT DO WE GOT, CHIEF?
"THAT ONE'S *ARISA HINES*, THE SOMEWHAT *RELUCTANT* LEADER'A BLUE TEAM.
"SHE *LOOKS* NORMAL ENOUGH, BUT SHE'S *PSYCHIC*. TELEPATHY, TELEKINESIS-- THAT SORTA STUFF."
HANK IN THE LEPIDOPTERRARIUM PICKED UP THIS SUDDEN DIMENSIONAL *BREACH* IN MASSACHUSETTS, ARISA. IT LOOKS LIKE AN ABANDONED *FACTORY* JUST OUTSIDE THE TOWN OF *NORTON*.
ABINGTON, FREETOWN, REHOBOTH-- THE *BRIDGEWATER* TRIANGLE. BIG IS GOING TO *LOVE* THIS. A LOT OF *WEIRD STUFF* HAS HAPPENED THERE.
"THAT ONE THEY JUST CALL *"MG"*. HIM I CAN'T FIGURE OUT-- HE'S A MYSTERY."
CHIEF. REQUEST YOU *REASSIGN* THIS ONE, SIR. RED TEAM IS *SCRAMBLED* AND *STANDING BY*. I HAVE TWO NEW *AGENTS* THAT I'D LIKE TO GET OUT IN THE *FIELD* AND SEE WHAT THEY'VE GOT.
"PETER HAMMERSKOLD. RECENTLY ACQUIRED FROM THE UNITED STATES MARINE CORPS. LEADER OF RED TEAM."
HERE WE GO...
I'VE ALSO LOGGED MORE HOURS IN THE FIELD THAN HINES AND, AS THIS IS STILL CLASSIFIED AN *"UNKNOWN"*, I FEEL THAT MY EXPERIENCE WOULD BE A GREAT ADVANTAGE.
"BELIEVES HE SHOULD BE LEADIN' BLUE TEAM. HE'S THE ONLY ONE."

BESIDES, SIR, RED TEAM IS ASSEMBLED AND READY TO DEPLOY IMMEDIATELY. BLUE TEAM ISN'T EVEN--
ARISA?
MM.
BIG IS ON HIS WAY UP FROM THE BIOLOGICS LAB. CHOOPIE IS...
OH, GREAT...
CHOOPIE IS ON HIS WAY.
I'M SORRY, PETER, BUT I'M GOING TO HAVE TO DENY THAT REQUEST. IT'S BECAUSE OF YOUR NOVICE AGENTS THAT I'D FEEL MORE COMFORTABLE SENDING BLUE TEAM ON THIS ONE.
TEE HEE!
WITH ALL DUE RESPECT, SIR, I'D LIKE TO VOLUNTEE--
WHAT ARE YOU LAUGHING AT, CASPER?!
"THE CUTE ONE? THAT'S MOLLY MACALLISTAR. SHE'S A GHOST. A REAL SWEETHEART."
OH. NOTHING. › SNICKER ‹
YEAH, NOTHING. › SNICKER ‹

SO THANKS ANYWAY, HAMMERSKOLD, FOR THAT ENCOURAGING VOTE OF CONFIDENCE, BUT I GUESS BLUE TEAM'LL HAVE TO DO WITHOUT YOUR EXPERIENCE AND EXPERTISE THIS TIME.
WHAT TEAM?! ALL I SEE IS YOU, THE BRAIN, AND THE GHOST! WHERE'S YOUR BLOOD-SUCKING PSYCHO AND THE BIG FURRY--
HELLO, PETER.
UH, ULP...
UH, HI...
...DOCTOR.
"BIG AS IN BIGFOOT! REALLY! THEY CAPTURED HIM YEARS AGO--
"AN' PUT HIM IN THIS EVOLVO-RAY THINGIE THEY GOT--A COUPLE'A TIMES...
"NOW HE'S TH SMARTEST STRONGES THING GOIN'
TAKE YOUR TEAM TO THE TRAINING WING, PETER. SEE "WHAT THEY'VE GOT" IN A LESS DANGEROUS SITUATION.
ALSO, YOU MIGHT WANNA TAK A FEW STEP TO YOUR LEFT...
THE DAY I START TAKING ADVICE FROM YOU, HINES, IS THE DAY I--
WHAT DO YOU MEAN "A FEW STEPS TO THE LEFT"?
GERONIMO, LARRY AND CURLY!
WHA--?
UH OH.
THUD!

'CAUSE CHOOPIE'S TOO SMALL FOR THE PNEUMATICS SO HE MAKES HIS OWN SHORTCUTS.
CHOOPIE! COME ON! LET'S GET GOING!
"EL CHUPACABRAS. THE MYTHICAL LATIN AMERICAN GOAT-SUCKER. THEY CAUGHT THIS ONE IN PUERTO RICO A FEW YEARS AGO AN' PUT 'IM THROUGH THAT EVOLVO-RAY LIKE THEY DID WITH BIG.
"DIDN'T WORK OUT QUITE THE SAME. Y'KNOW, S'LIKE THEY SAY...
"INDIVIDUAL RESULTS MAY VARY."
C'MERE, YOU LITTLE--
GOTTA GO!
AND YOU KNOW THERE'S NO FOOD OR BEVERAGES ON THE SKIPPER.
HERE. HOLD THIS.
?
WHAT-- WHAT IS THIS?! YOU BETTER NOT HAVE--
IS THIS BLOOD?!?
NO, IT'S COKE. YOU CAN HAVE IT.
PLUTT
WELL...
THERE'S A LITTLE BLOOD IN IT.

LISTEN, UH...GUYS...?
WHEN WE LAND, UH...I THINK WE SHOULD STICK TOGETHER.
I DON'T THINK IT'D BE GOOD TO GET TOO FAR AWAY UNTIL WE'VE GOT AN IDEA WHAT WE'RE DEALING WITH.
'KAY...?
ARISA, YOU'RE TEAM LEADER. JUST TELL US WHAT YOU WANT US TO DO. YOU'RE DOING FINE.
OKAY, MOLLY--SCOUT THE PLACE OUT-- SEE IF YOU CAN FIND WHATEVER IT IS WE'RE SUPPOSED TO BE LOOKING FOR. IF YOU DO, DON'T MAKE CONTACT. TRY NOT TO BE SEEN--WE DON'T WANNA SPOOK IT.
THE REST OF US WILL QUIETLY STAY OUT HERE AND WAIT QUIETLY 'TIL SHE GETS BACK AND THEN QUIETLY DECIDE WHAT TO DO WHEN WE'VE GOT A BETTER IDEA OF WHAT'S GOING ON.
WOO HOO! WE'RE GONNA--
CHOOPIE! WHAT WORD DID I JUST SAY THREE TIMES VERY CLEARLY AND SUCCINCTLY ESPECIALLY FOR YOU?
I KNOW...
QUIETLY.
UM, ARISA...
OOPS. SORRY...
DEET DEET
...ALMOST FORGOT.

blue ribbon laundry
OKAY. SCOUT AHEAD. TRY NOT TO BE SEEN. DON'T SCARE IT.
BUT WHAT IF I'M SCARED...?
'CAUSE I AM.
JUST 'CAUSE I'M, LIKE, INTANGIBLE DOESN'T MEAN THAT I DON'T GET--
ARE YOU PICKING UP THE BREACH AT ALL?
NO. IT MUST'VE CLOSED UP BEHIND IT WHENEVER WHATEVER IT IS CAME THROUGH. BUT I AM ONLY READING ONE OTHER BIOSIGNATURE BESIDES US, SO WHATEVER IT IS, IT CAME THROUGH ALO--
ARISA...
...I SMELL BLOOD.
OH! IT'S...
...THAT'S...
...GROSS!

ARISA! IT'S IN THERE! AND, IT'S, LIKE, HUGE! IT--
HURRRRRR
WHOA!
OKAYYY...
...ASIDE FROM PISSED, I HAVE ABSOLUTELY NO IDEA WHAT THAT THING IS.

I'M GONNA GO WITH "HOSTILE". MG--HIT IT WITH THE PLASMA-NET.
GOT IT.
THOOOT
HREEE
HREEE
HREEE
DID...DID I JUST SEE THAT?
DID THAT THING JUST HYDRA ON US...?
IT...MORPHED...
...INTO MANY SHAPES...
...TO LET THE NET PASS RIGHT THROUGH IT...
...BUT IT'S BACK TO ONE NOW...
HURRRR

MOLLY--GO HIGH!
TRY TO DISTRACT IT WHILE, CHOOP, YOU TRY TO GET IN LOW WITH THAT TRANQ GUN.
AND, CHOOPIE, WATCH OUT FOR IT'S--
HUH?
...TAIL!
WAP
OKAY, WE'RE GETTING NOWHERE WITH THE PHYSICAL--TIME TO SEE IF A PSYCHIC ATTACK'LL TAKE DOWN THIS HORRORSHOW...!
...NOT THAT I HAVE ANY DESIRE TO GET INTO THIS THING'S HEAD...
...UNGH! FIGHTING ME...IT'S...
...NO!
UHNN!
NO!
ARISA!!

ARE...ARE YOU ALRIGHT...? I...I JUST...
WHAT DO WE DO? WHAT DO WE DO?! WE'RE GETTING FLATTENED BY THIS THING!
OH!
HUNF!
KRACK!
OH, NO YOU DITN'T!!
DON'T TELL ME YOU JUST JAW-CRUNCHED MY BEST FRIEND BIG!!! NOW YOU ASKED FOR IT, YOU BIG...FREAKY... WHATEVER-YOU-ARE!
FFFFTTTT!
PPPT!
WHADDAYA GOT TO THAY NOW, YOU THTUPID THONUVVA--
OH, THIT-

CHOOPIE--LET GO! DETACH! DETA--
HURRRR!
AAHHHH-
THUD
OUTH!
THAWWEE.
CHOOPIE! I GOT YA! GO LIMP! GO--
NOW WHAT?
--OOF!
WHAT IS THAT THING?
DUNNO.
THAT THING TOOK, LIKE, FIVE GOOD PUNCHES FROM BIG! IF IT CAN SURVIVE THAT, THEN THE ONLY WAY YOU'RE GONNA STOP IT IS IF YOU DROP A HOUSE ON IT OR SOMETHING!

HMM.
WHAT?
REMEMBER THOSE CEMENT-EATING SLUGS THAT YOU BROUGHT BACK FROM THAT BASE DIMENSION ABOUT A MONTH AND A HALF AGO?
YEAH...
GIVEN THE RATE AT WHICH THEY EAT THROUGH A YARD OF MORTAR...ALONG WITH THEIR RATE OF REPRODUCTION... AND THE SIZE OF THIS BUILDING--
IF WE WERE TO SEND KARL BACK IN TIME TO DROP 6 OF THEM OFF HERE, LET'S SEE... EXACTLY 35-POINT-6 YEARS AGO--
--THEY SHOULD HAVE THE ENTIRE STRUCTURE COMPLETELY UNSTABLE...
TAK TAK TAK
...RIIIIIGHT....ABOOOOUT...

krkk
krkkk
...NOW.
krkk
kusssh
SHOOOOMMM!
YEAH, BUT, LIKE...
...YOU GUYS...
...WHAT IF THEY DON'T LET US DO THAT?

"SO THAT'S BASICALLY WHAT THEY DO. WHEN SOMETHIN'AT DOESN'T BELONG HERE SHOWS UP, THESE GUYS PACK ITS BAGS AN' SEND 'EM HOME.
"'CEPT WHEN THEY CAN'T."
THIS ONE FER EXAMPLE, THEY DON'T KNOW WHERE IT CAME FROM SO THEY BRING 'EM BACK HERE T'BEDLAM AN' PUT 'EM IN A CONTAINMENT CELL 'TIL THEY CAN FIGURE OUT WHAT TA DO WITH 'IM.
A CONTAINMENT CELL THEY THOUGHT WAS GONNA HOLD 'IM...
BUT...

...THEY WERE WRONG.
Next Issue:
THE NEW PERHAPANAUTS

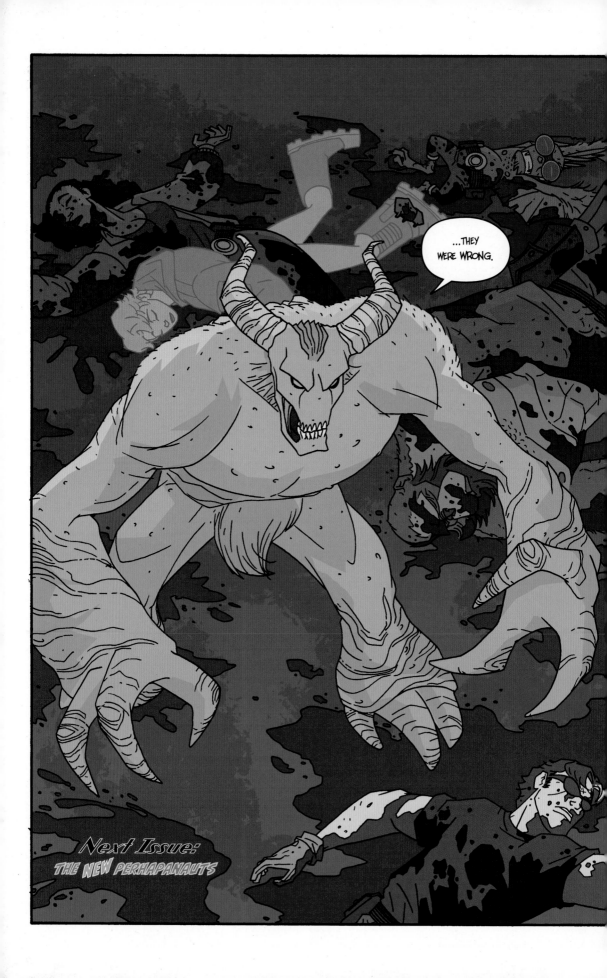

CHAPTER TWO

ARE WE THERE YET?
ARE WE THERE YET?
ARE WE THERE YET?
ARE WE TH--
CHOOPIE!
BUT I CAN'T WAIT ANYMORE. I GOTTA--
YOU GOTTA STAY IN YOUR SEAT AND KEEP THAT BELT BUCKLED UNTIL WE'RE BACK IN THE BAY AND HAVE COME TO A COMPLETE--
...STOP! CHOOPIE!
CAN'T STOP! CAN'T WAIT!
CAN'T FIGHT IT! THE URGE IS TOO--
OUTTA THE WAY, CHUMPS! THIS IS AN EMERGENCY!
CAN'T HOLD IT BACK ANY LONGER!
THIS CHOOPIE'S GOTTA--

TODD AND CRAIG'S
Perhapanauts
in
"adaptability"
WORDS--TODD
PICTURES--CRAIG
COLORS
--RICO
...EAT!!
AH...
...HEAVEN.
HELLO, BABIES...
...I'VE MISSED YOU...

I STILL DON'T GET IT.
IT'S REALLY SIMPLE, MOL. SEE, THEY MUST HAVE LET US DO IT, BECAUSE IT'S ALREADY HAPPENED. NOW ALL WE HAVE TO DO IS ASK THEM.
AND WE KNOW THEY'RE GOING TO SAY YES, BECAUSE WE ALREADY SAW IT HAPPEN IN THE PAST.
MY HEAD HURTS.
BUT, LIKE, AT LEAST WE GOT THAT THING DOWN! YOU'RE DOING A GREAT JOB AS TEAM LEADER, 'RIS!
I DID AN "OKAY" JOB. A GREAT TEAM LEADER WOULDN'T'VE LET ANY OF HER TEAM GET TAGGED. THAT THING GOT A PIECE OF EVERYBODY ...EXCEPT YOU.
IT EVEN HAD SOME KIND OF PSYCHIC BLOCKER UP AGAINST ME.
ANYWAY, DIDJA NOTICE THE NEW GUY? HOW WORRIED HE GOT WHEN HE THOUGHT YOU WERE HURT?
I THINK, LIKE, MAYBE THE NEW GUY'S STARTING TO CRUSH ON THE TEAM LEADER.
I AM SURE THAT'S NOT TRUE.

...IT WOULD BE NARROW-MINDED OF ME TO IMAGINE THAT WE'VE CATEGORIZED EVEN A FRACTION OF WHAT'S OUT THERE...
...BUT I'VE CROSS-REFERENCED ALL IT'S APPARENT ATTRIBUTES AGAINST ALL OF BEDLAM'S FILES AND CAN'T FIND A LISTING THAT COMES EVEN CLOSE TO THAT CREATURE'S DESCRIPTION.
HMMM.
I'VE NEVER SEEN ANYTHING LIKE IT. IT ALLOWED MY PLASMA-NET TO PASS RIGHT THROUGH IT, DEFLECTED ARISA'S PSYCHIC ATTACK BACK AT HER...
FOR A MOMENT DURING THE SKIRMISH I HAD THE SENSATION THAT IT WASN'T SIMPLY A RAGING BEAST LASHING OUT, BUT THAT IT WAS... MEASURING US... THINKING...
HOW DO YOU KNOW WHAT HE'S THINKING? BOTH YOU AND JOANN SAID THAT NEITHER ONE OF YOU CAN READ HIM. HE'S JUST GRAY NOISE, ISN'T THAT WHAT YOU TOLD ME? SO, LIKE, YA NEVER KNOW...
...HE COULD BE CRUSHING ON YOU.
SHLURP!
HE ISN'T.
'KAY, MAYBE NOT...
HE IS CUTE THOUGH.
THE PART THAT FASCINATES ME MOST, THOUGH, IS THE PHENOMENON WITH THE NET. I WOULD HAVE THOUGHT I WAS HALLUCINATING IF YOU HADN'T WITNESSED IT AS WELL.
MOLLY!
› GIGGLE! ‹
YEAH, THAT WAS DISTURBING, I--
WHAT ARE THEY DOING?
OH, YEAH, THAT. THAT CAN BE A BIT DISCONCERTING AT FIRST. TELEPATHIC CONVERSATION. CHOOPIE AND I CALL IT "GIRL TALK". ALL WE GET TO HEAR ARE RANDOM GASPS AND GIGGLES. YOU GET USED TO IT.

"I'VE WONDERED WHY ARISA DOESN'T USE HER TELEPATHY TO TALK TO US IN THE FIELD. IT WOULD BE SO MUCH EASIER THAN THE RADIOS."
"BOTH ARISA AND JOANN FEEL THAT IT'S A VIOLATION TO PUSH THEIR WAY INTO SOME-ONE'S MIND UNINVITED. ON ANY LEVEL. IT'S A TRUST ISSUE. A SORT OF 'TELEPATH'S CODE OF HONOR'."
ASIDE FROM A CURSORY SCAN OF SOMEONE'S AURA, THEY DON'T DELVE. PEOPLE CAN BE EXTREMELY PROTECTIVE OF THEIR PRIVACY...
--HAVE YOU NOTICED THAT?
BUT HE'S, LIKE, SUCH A MYSTERY, Y'KNOW? I MEAN, WHAT'S UP WITH THAT?
THE ONLY REASON HE'S HERE IS BECAUSE THE CHIEF ASSURED HIM THAT NO ONE AT BEDLAM WOULD TRY TO FIND OUTWHO HE WAS. NO BACKGROUND CHECKS, NO MEDICAL EXAMS...
I MEAN, I LIKE HIM AND ALL. HE'S SEEMS LIKE A REALLY NICE GUY...
...BUT WHAT'S HE HIDING?
UM... YEAH, I... UM...
...
...SO, WHAT DO WE THINK THIS THING WAS?

SO, WHAT DO WE THINK THIS THING *IS?*
DUNNO. BLUE TEAM BROUGHT IT IN AN ***HOUR*** AGO AND THEY--
WAITAMINNIT. ***BLUE*** TEAM? WHICH ONE'S ***THAT?*** IZZAT THE ONE WITH THE ***PSYCHIC*** CHICK AND--
YEAH. YEAH. THE ONE ***BIGFOOT*** IS ON.
OH. YEAH. GOOD. I LIKE THEM.
YEAH, ME TOO.
"ANYWAY, TAC BROUGHT IT IN WRAPPED IN ENOUGH ***S.N.O.T.**** TO CHOKE A...A... YOU KNOW, SOMETHING ***BIG!***
"SAID THAT IT REALLY GAVE 'EM A ROUGH TIME. ALMOST TOOK THE ***WHOLE TEAM*** DOWN!"
"WOW."
* SENTIENT NANO-ORGANISM TECHNOLOGY--DAVE
"YEAH. SO ANYWAY, 'TIL THEY FIGURE OUT WHAT IT IS, WE GOT ORDERS TO KEEP IT IN THE STRONGEST ***HIBERNATION SOLUTION*** WE GOT!
"THAT, MY FRIEND, IS ***HS14***."
"BELIEVE ***ME,*** MAN...
"...THAT IS ***ONE*** MONSTER THAT AIN'T GONNA BE WAKIN' UP ANYTIME ***SOON!***"

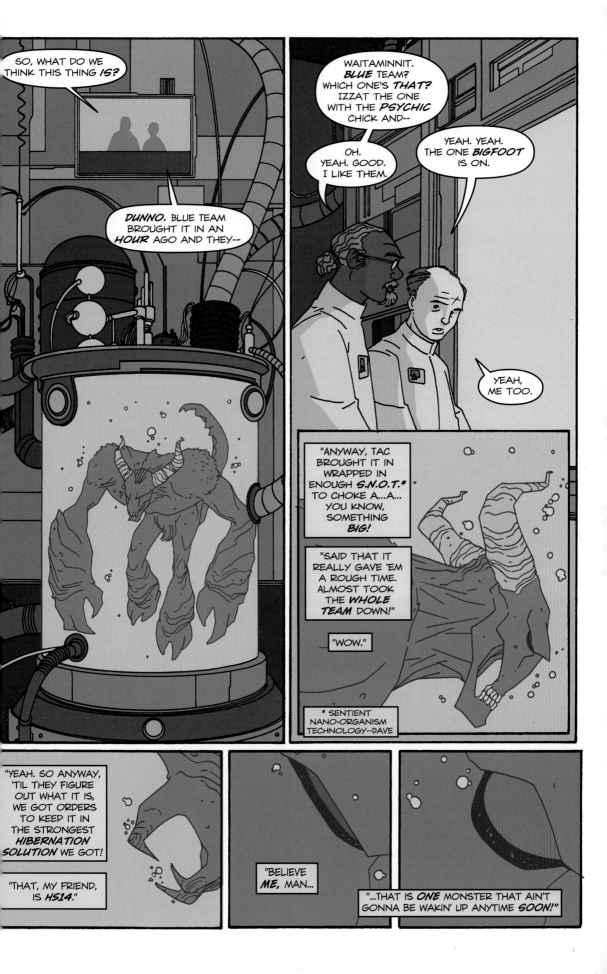

SO, WHAT ARE YOU BOYS UP TO?
WE'RE RUNNING ALL THE FILES TO SEE IF WE CAN DETERMINE WHAT THAT *THING* WAS WE RAN AFOUL OF THIS EVENING.
BUT WE HAVE *NOTHING* THAT INCLUDES *REPELLING* YOUR PSYCHIC ASSAULT OR *DISINTEGRATING* INTO SMALLER VERSIONS TO ESCAPE CAPTURE.
BUT NOT JUST SMALLER *VERSIONS* OF ITSELF. WHEN IT...*MORPHED*...I'M *SURE* I SAW THE FACES OF *OTHER* ANIMALS IN THERE...A *LION*...AND A *DRAGON*...
...AND A...*GOAT*...?
HMMM.
?
DID SOMEBODY SAY *"GOAT"*?!
GO BACK TO YOUR SHOW, CHOOPIE.
THE HEADS OF A LION, A SERPENT, AND A GOAT... OF COURSE.
I SHOULD HAVE *SEEN* IT! THE GREEK *MYTH!* BELLEPHERON SLEW--
TAK TAK TAK TAK

RIGHT! THE CHIMAERA!
THE ORIGINAL SHAPE-CHANGER. APPARENTLY WITH THE ABILITY TO ADAPT TO ANY OBSTACLE OR ENVIRONMENT IT MIGHT POSSIBLY ENCOUNTER.
BUT WAIT. WAIT! THE GREEK MYTHS WERE... MYTHS! THOSE CREATURES WERE FANTASY! LEGENDS! THEY DIDN'T REALLY EXIST!
OH.
RIGHT.
OKAY...
I GET IT.
BUT, LIKE, YOU GUYS...
WELL...
I MEAN, I KNOW I'M NOT VERY GOOD AT THIS STUFF, BUT...I HAVE A QUESTION...

"I MEAN, IF THIS GREEK MYTHY THING IS THE ULTIMATE SHAPE-CHANGER...
"...AND IT CAN ADAPT ITSELF TO, LIKE, ANYTHING IT COMES UP AGAINST...
"I DON'T KNOW, BUT WOULDN'T THAT MEAN THAT, LIKE, IT COULD ADAPT ITSELF...
blue team quarters
...RIGHT OUT OF THAT CONTAINMENT FLUID HE'S SOAKING IN?
OH--
CRAP.

THOOOM!
UFF!
CHOOP'S
KEEP OUT!
WAMMM!
HURRR!
NGH--*
crasssh!

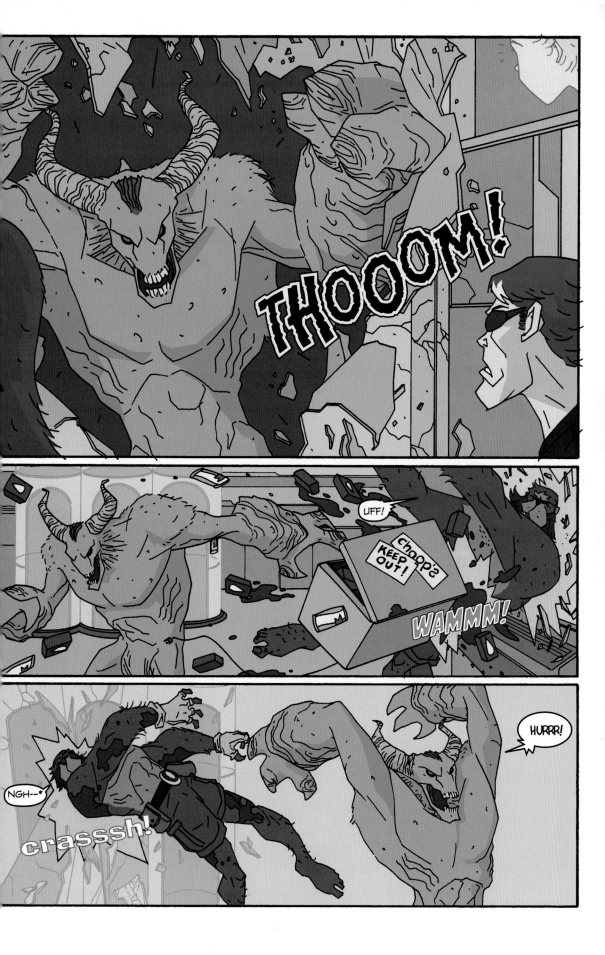

HEY! WHAT--?
WHAMM!
klussh
UNNT--
ARISA?! QUICK--PSY-FRY IT BEFORE IT CAN--
NO...NO. NONE...OF THAT.
...
IT... IT TALKS--
HURR!
HUHH!
THUDD!
UNGH!

LAST ONE LEFT... THE GHOST.
NO.
I HAVE... SOMETHING... FOR...YOU.
SWATTT
AHHHH--
HA...HA...HA...HA...HA...

OOOH... THAT HURT.
I HAVEN'T HURT IN-
'RIS?
COME ON, ARISA. YA GOTTA WAKE UP.
COME ON! YA GOTTA, LIKE, HELP ME HERE.
ANYTIME, 'RIS.
PLEASE...?
I DON'T KNOW IF I CAN DO THIS BY MYSELF.

AHHHHHHH!
COME ON, ARISA! WAKE UP! WAKE UP!
FUMPP
HURRM--
ARISA? COME ON, GIRLFRIEND! YA GOTTA GET UP! I DON'T KNOW WHAT TO DO NOW!
UHHN... ...M-MOL?
MOLLY? MOLLY, WHAT'S HAPPENING?
I KNOCKED IT OUT, 'RIS-- WITH CHOOPIE'S STUN GUN...
...MAH... MESS-YOU-UP GUN...
...BUT IT'S NOT GONNA STAY DOWN FOR LONG! WE GOTTA DO SOMETHING NOW, 'RIS! MG IS OUT AND I THINK BIG IS HURT REAL BAD!

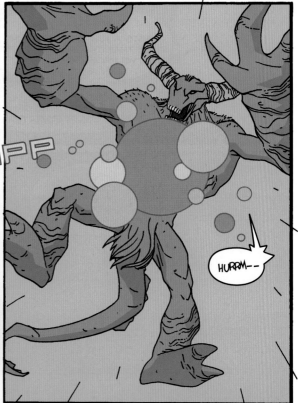

UHHHN... THE...STUN ONLY LASTS A FEW MINUTES...AND SINCE THAT THING CAN ADAPT... WE PROBABLY DON'T EVEN HAVE THAT.
OUR PRIORITY IS GET BIG TO THE MEDLAB. IF WE CAN GET HIM INTO A PNEUMATIC...
NNFF! HE'S...TOO HEAVY. I COULD LIFT HIM WITH TK IF MY HEAD WASN'T STILL SPINNING...
I...I COULD GO INTO HIM... "POSSESS" HIM LIKE I DID TO YOU, BUT--
WAIT!
CHOOP'S
KEEP OUT!
MG!
MOLLY... COULD YOU POSSESS...
...THE CHIMAERA?
I...I COULD... BUT...ONLY IF IT WAS UNCONSCIOUS. OTHERWISE, IT WOULD FIGHT ME FOR CONTROL AND...
...AND I... I DON'T THINK I COULD--
YOU WON'T HAVE TO, MOL--
--I WILL.

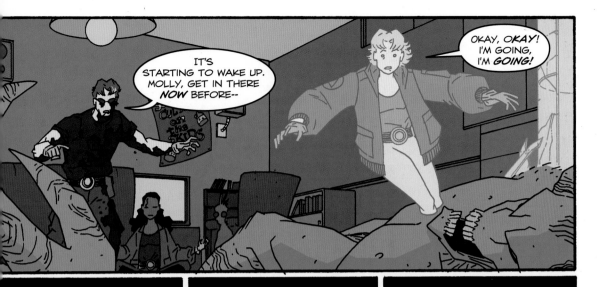

IT'S STARTING TO WAKE UP. MOLLY, GET IN THERE *NOW* BEFORE--

OKAY, *OKAY!* I'M GOING, I'M *GOING!*

YOU? THE SHADE?! DO YOU BELIEVE I'M GOING TO ALLOW YOU, THE MERE ECHO OF A HUMAN, TO DETER ME FOR EVEN A FRACTION OF A SECOND? DON'T YOU KNOW THAT IN HERE, GIRL, I'M THE BOSS? THAT IN HERE, YOU'RE NOT UNTOUCHABLE? THAT I CAN TEAR YOU LIMB FROM LIMB?!

AND I'M GOING TO.

VERY SLOWLY.

TILL YOU FORGET HOW TO SCREAM...

GET AWAY FROM HER, YOU...

THOOOOOOOM

...SLIME!

MOLLY! GO!

GOOD THINKIN', EINSTEIN. LETTIN' ARISA GO. HE'S TOO BIG. WE'RE NEVER GONNA LIFT HIM.
HMM. MAYBE WE CAN'T, BUT...
HEY, MOLLY-- CAN YOU GIVE US A HAND OVER HERE?
SURE... I MEAN...
...SURE.
SO...THE TELEPATH. IN MY DAY YOU WOULD HAVE SIMPLY BEEN CALLED "WITCH". I'VE BEEN AROUND SINCE THE BEGINNING OF TIME, WITCH. I HAVE COMMITTED ATROCITIES YOU WOULD NOT CONCEIVE IN A HUNDRED LIFETIMES. I HAVE A MILLENNIA OF EXPERIENCE TO CALL UPON.
ARE YOU SURE YOU'RE READY TO THROW DOWN WITH ME?
YOU DARED TO COME AND CONFRONT ME HERE, WITCH?!
IN MY MIND?!
IN MY PSYCHE?!
IN MY REALM?!

I THINK HE'S BEGINNING TO, LIKE, COME AROUND, M.
THAT'S A GOOD SIGN, MOL, BUT LET'S GET HIM TO THE MEDLAB AS QUICK AS WE CAN ANYWAY. WE DON'T KNOW HOW LONG ARISA CAN HOLD OUT IN THERE.
HUNNH...
CHOOPIE, YOU STILL GOT IT COVERED?
COVERED.
WHAT THE HELL IS GOING ON HERE?!
WE'VE GOT TWO MEN DOWN IN CONTAINMENT, THREE MORE IN TECH, SECURITY SAYS THAT BLUE QUARTERS HAS BEEN TOTALLED AND YOU'RE TAKING THE MOST DANGEROUS CREATURE WE'VE EVER ENCOUNTERED FOR A WALK?!
NOT NOW, HAMMERSKOLD!
WHAT HAPPENED HERE? WHERE'S HINES?
THIS THING GOT LOOSE. ARISA IS DEEP INSIDE IT'S BRAIN TRYING DESPERATELY TO KEEP IT RESTRAINED UNTIL WE CAN BLOW IT INTO ANOTHER DIMENSION.
WE'VE GOT IT UNDER CONTROL. NOW PLEASE GET OUT OF OUR WAY AND LET US GET BIG TO THE MEDLAB.
LISTEN, NEW GUY, I DON'T TAKE ORDERS FROM YOU. I--
CHOOPIE...
WHOA.
FINE. GO. WHEN YOU BLUES SCREW IT UP, RED TEAM WILL COME IN AND CLEAN IT UP.
WHAT IDIOT GAVE THAT LITTLE FREAK A GUN...?

I KNOW OF HORRORS SO ALIEN AND BIZARRE THAT THEY WILL HAVE YOU SCRAPING TO HOLD ONTO YOUR SANITY!
OOZING, SLITHERING, PRIMORDIAL CREATURES THAT CRAWLED THIS PLANE BEFORE THE SHAPE OF THINGS WAS SET!
NOTHING TO SAY, WITCH? HAS THIS ALL BEEN TOO MUCH FOR YOUR FRAGILE LITTLE MIND?
WELL...
AWWK!
FOOOM
HOW'S THIS?
"MILLENNIA" IS PLURAL.
YOU CAN HAVE "A MILLENNIUM" OR "MILLENNIUMS", BUT YOU CAN'T HAVE "A MILLENNIA". THAT'S LIKE SAYING YOU HAVE "A TEETH".
IT'S SIMPLE GRAMMAR, STUPID. LOOK IT UP.

BIG, YOU REALLY SHOULD BE LYING DOWN, Y'KNOW. THAT WAS, LIKE, A MAJOR CRACK ON THE HEAD AND YOU DID LOSE A LOT OF BLOOD.
I'M GOOD ENOUGH TO FLIP A SWITCH.
HE KNOWS WHAT HE'S DOING?
YEAH, HE DOES.
YOU DO KNOW WHAT YOU'RE DOING, RIGHT, M?
YEAH. DON'T WORRY, YOU GUYS. THIS SHOULD WORK PERFECTLY.
OKAY, MOLLY. TELL ARISA THAT YOU GUYS CAN GET OUT NOW.
AND TELL ARISA TO LISTEN FOR ME.
GOT IT, M. LIKE, GOOD LUCK.
ARISA...?
MG SAYS "NOW".
THANKS, MOL.
BYE, YOU UGLY FREAK.
WHA--

WHERE?
AHH... THE IN-BETWEENER.
THEY DON'T KNOW WHAT YOU REALLY ARE, DO THEY?
NO MATTER.
I WILL PEEL YOUR FLESH AND SHOW THEM WHAT YOU REALLY ARE.
AND THEN, ONCE I'M DONE WITH YOU, I WILL MOVE THROUGH THIS ENTIRE FACILITY, AND OPEN THEM ALL UP--
--JUST TO SEE WHAT'S INSIDE.
SWISH!
ARISA-- CAN YOU HEAR ME?
YES, MG.
TELL BIG WHEN TO CLOSE IT.
NOW?

I CAN SMELL YOUR FEAR. YOU THINK YOU CAN EVADE ME. BUT NOT BEFORE I TEAR YOU TO SHREDS.
JUST WAIT...
NOT UNTIL IT'S ALL THE WAY THROUGH...
NOT... YET...
NOT...
CLICK
ZZZZZIMMMMM
RAAAAAAART--
NO!
SSHUCK!
CHOOPIE! WHAT DID YOU DO?! YOU...YOU KILLED IT!
ISN'T THAT WHAT WE WERE GONNA DO?
NO! WE WERE GOING TO LET MG LURE IT INTO THAT POCKET DIMENSION HE CREATED AND TRAP IT THERE! BUT YOU...YOU CUT IT IN TWO!
I DON'T REALLY HAVE A PROBLEM WITH THAT.
WELL, WE HAVE A PROBLEM...
MG HASN'T COME BACK.
NEXT ISSUE: MG COMES BACK.

CHAPTERTHREE

C! nico.

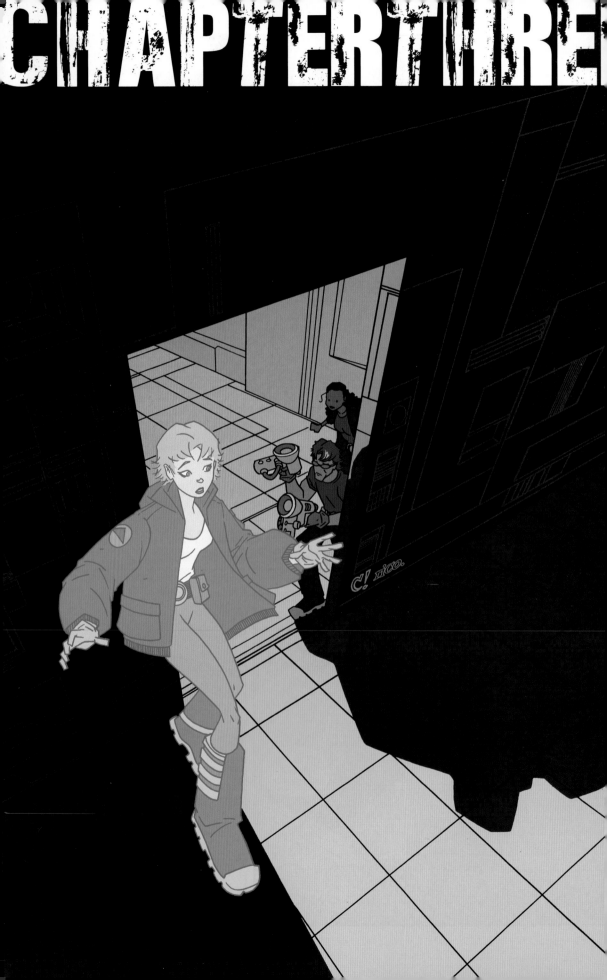

WHERE? AHH, THE IN-BETWEENER.
THEY DON'T KNOW WHAT YOU REALLY ARE, DO THEY?
NO MATTER. I WILL PEEL THE FLESH FROM YOUR BONES AND SHOW THEM WHAT YOU REALLY ARE.
ARISA, CAN YOU HEAR ME?
I'M RIGHT HERE, MG.
TELL BIG TO GET READY.
NOT YET...
...NOT...
...YET...
HURRARRRRR!
CLICK
ZZZZIMMMMM
--RRAAIIIIEEEEEEEEE!
NO!

CHOOPIE! WHAT DID YOU DO? YOU...YOU KILLED IT!
WHAT? I THOUGHT THAT'S WHAT WE WERE GONNA DO.
NO! NO, NO! MG WAS GOING TO LURE IT INTO THAT POCKET DIMENSION AND WE WERE GOING TO TRAP IT THERE UNTIL WE FIGURED OUT WHAT TO DO WITH IT!
OH.
THAT'S A GOOD IDEA, TOO.
MG WAS GOING TO "FLIP" BACK*--
--THE ONLY PROBLEM IS...
...HE HASN'T COME BACK.
* EDITOR'S NOTE--USING HIS UNCANNY ABILITY TO "SLIDE" BETWEEN DIMENSIONS --DAVE
TODD AND CRAIG'S
Perhapanauts
IN
"getting closure"
WORDS--TODD PICTURES--CRAIG COLORS--RICO

NO... NO! I WASN'T READY. HE WASN'T THROUGH!
BISECTED. WHAT CAN I DO FOR HIM?
NOTHING.
I--
AROOOOOO!
HUH? WHAT WAS THA--
ARRROOOOOOOOO!
ONE OF THE LOCALS. GREAT.
I BROUGHT THE CHIMAERA TO THIS HOSTILE WORLD BECAUSE HE WAS HOSTILE, BUT NOW I'M WOND--
grab!
AAHHHRRRRRRR!

YOU... HRUK...BEAT ME... IN...BETWEENER... HRUKK...
BUT I...
HRUKKK...KNOW OF YOUR...KIND...
I KNOW THAT...YOU CAN ONLY MOVE BETWEEN THE DIMENSIONS S-SOLO...THAT YOU...HRUKKKK... CANNOT BEAR A...PASSENGER.
THAT TO DO SO WOULD...HRUKKKK... T-TEAR YOU APART...
SO YOU MAY...MARK MY DEFEAT...
BUT I GO, CLAIMING ONE... LAST...
...VICTIM.
HE'S RIGHT. CAUGHT IN HIS DEATH-GRIP LIKE THIS, I'M NOT GOING ANYWHERE...
...
ARROOOOOOOT!
AND WITH THAT CREATURE APPROACHING, I'M LIKE A GOAT STAKED OUT FOR SACRIFI--
HUH?--
RRONK!?
WHAT ARE THOSE THINGS?!

SCORES OF THEM...
ARRROOWWWWW!
SWARMING ALL OVER IT...
ROOOOT-
SKRIP!
SKRAPPT!
RRIPP!
...WHICH, AT FIRST GLANCE, I'M SURE SEEMS LIKE A LUCKY BREAK FOR ME.
UNLESS...
BIG, HURRY! WE'VE GOTTA DO SOMETHING!
WHY CAN'T WE JUST HIT THE "OPEN GATE" BUTTON? THAT WORKS ANY OTHER TIME.
BUT NOT THIS TIME, ARISA. MG BUILT THIS PROGRAM ON THE FLY, PLANNING A ONE-WAY-ONLY TRIP FOR THAT THING. IT'S A GATE TO A VERY HOSTILE DIMENSION.
HE DIDN'T WANT TO ALLOW THE POSSIBILITY THAT SOMEONE MIGHT INADVERTENTLY COME ALONG AND OPEN IT BACK UP.
IF I ONLY HAD THE COORDINATES...
TAK TAK TAK TAK

...UNLESS, OF COURSE, THEY'RE STILL HUNGRY...
...WHICH THEY ARE.
sniff sniff
AND I'M DESSERT, UNLESS...
SSSSKRAAAAAPE
HMM.
WHAT? WHAT?!
HE DID HAVE TIME TO BUILD A BACK DOOR INTO THE PROGRAM, BUT I CAN'T GET IN WITHOUT THE PROPER PASSWORD.
I'M TRYING ALL OUR USUALS, BUT...
HEY! Z'ANYBODY SEEN MY MESS-YOU-UP GUN?
SSKUMP

CHIMAERA? BEDLAM? SOUTHERN CULTURE ON THE SKIDS?
NO, NO, AND NO.
COME ON, M-- WHAT WERE YOU THINKING?...
"WHAT WAS IN YOUR HEAD?"
I GOT IT. I GOT IT!
"ARISA! IT'S 'ARISA!'"
...
WHAT?!
FUMPP
IT'S "ARISA".
JUST TRY IT. COME ON!
password: aris_
TAK
TAK
TAK
THAT'S IT! ARISA, GET OVER TO THE PODIUM. I'LL INITIATE THE COORDINATES AND LET YOU KNOW WHEN IT'S PRIMED FOR YOU TO OPEN THE GATE.
GOTCHA!

THIS IS MADDENING-- WATCHING THEM GET CLOSER AND CLOS--
SKRRIP
RRIP
RRIP
NEEE NEEE NEEE NEEE NEEE NEEE
WHA--? OH, NO! THE GATE!
BIG MUST'VE ACCESSED THE PROGRAM! BUT THEY CAN'T!
IF THEY OPEN THE GATE, THESE THINGS WILL CHEW THEM TO PIECES BEFORE THEY EVEN KNOW WHAT HIT THEM!
HAVE TO GET BACK AND STOP THEM! COME ON, YOU LITTLE BUGGERS--EAT! EAT!
APERATURE INITIATED FOR OPENING IN 9 SECONDS
COME ON...
FUMPP FUMPP FUMPP
COME ON...!
JUST A LITTLE MORE! JUST A LITTLE...

...NOW!
NNNN--
3...2...1...
OKAY, ARISA--YOU CAN OPEN THE GATE N--
--NOOOO!
HEY! MY GUN!
HUNFFF

SORRY.
THERE...THERE WAS SOMETHING BAD ON THE OTHER SIDE OF THE...
IT'S OKAY. I...
M! WE WERE SO WORRIED ABOUT YOU AND--
OMIGOD! M! YOUR LEG! IT'S--
WE'VE GOTTA GET YOU DOWN TO THE MED-LAB AND HAVE DR. DAS--
NO...NO. I'M OKAY.
I'LL... BE ALL RIGHT.
I CAN TAKE CARE OF THIS MYSELF.
UM...
...S-SEE YA.
Y'KNOW, SOMETIMES...
...THAT IS ONE WEIRD GUY.
end

TODD AND CRAIG'S
Perhapanauts
IN
the TERROR from WITHIN!
TODD--WORDS CRAIG--PICTURES
RICO--COLORS
...TO TRAIN MORE AS A TEA--
OMIGOD! WHAT--?
THEY'RE IN SHOCK. ALMOST CATATONIC. THEY LOOK--
TERRIFIED.
WHAT HAPPENED HERE? WHAT COULD'VE--
KEITH!
KEITH--WHAT HAPPENED? WHERE'S HAMMERSKOLD? AND THE REST OF RED TEAM?
WERE IN...TRAINING WING... DIDN'T KNOW HE WAS IN THERE... HAMMERSKOLD WAS... TENSE, YELLED AT HIM, SAID THE WRONG THING...
...THEN THERE WAS JUST... SCREAMING. THEY WERE SCREAMING... WE WERE ALL SCREAMING...

WHO, SCRUFF? WHO DIDN'T YOU KNOW WAS IN THERE?
HIS EYES... THOSE EYES... IT WAS...
HIM...
IT WAS KARL.
DON'T...ARISA, DON'T LET THEM PUT ME IN THERE. IT'S TOO SMALL! TIGHT! I CAN'T BREATHE! I CAN'T BRE--
SHHH. IT'S OKAY, SCRUFFY. HERE. REST.
OKAY, YOU GUYS-- THIS IS WHAT WE'RE GONNA DO. MOLLY AND I ARE GONNA GO IN AND TRY TO TALK TO HIM; SHE'S THE CLOSEST THING HE'S GOT TO A FRIEND IN THIS PLACE.
MG, YOU GO GET JOANN. WE'RE DEFINITELY GONNA NEED HER FOR BACKUP ON THIS, AND SHE'S DONE A LOT OF WORK WITH HIM. BIG...
I'LL TELL YA WHAT THAT FREAK NEEDS IS A GOOD, OLD-FASHIONED KICK IN THE--
BIG, PLEASE ESCORT CHOOPIE BACK TO THE FAMILY ROOM. AND KEEP HIM THERE. THE ONLY HELP HE'D BE IS TO MAKE MATTERS WORSE.
HEY! WHADID I DO? WHY CAN'T I--
WHAT, YOU THINK I DON'T KNOW WHAT YOU DO TO HIM? YOU SHOULD BE ASHAMED OF YOURSELF.

SOON...
GREAT. WHEN HE ATTACKED THORNTON THEY PROBABLY BLEW THE POWER IN THE ENTIRE WING.
KARL?
KAAARRL!
ARE YOU OKAY WITH THIS, MOL? I'M SORRY THAT I JUST SORTA VOLUNTEERED YOU WITHOUT CHECKING WITH YOU FIRST.
N-NO, IT'S OKAY, 'RIS. LIKE, IT MAKES SENSE FOR ME TO BE THE SCOUT. 'SPECIALLY WHEN IT'S SOMETHING THAT'S, YOU KNOW...
...POTENTIALLY DANGEROUS.
DOESN'T MEAN I'M NOT...NERVOUS, THOUGH.
DR. SHEEHAN SAYS THAT THEY CAN EMANATE FEAR, THAT THEY CAN, LIKE, PROJECT AN AURA OF PURE TERROR.
SHE SAID THAT IT CAN EITHER BE THIS VAGUE, UNFOCUSED DREAD, OR IT CAN CALL UP YOUR DEEPEST, DARKEST NIGHTMA--
MOLLY MACALLISTAR
1986-2003
"GONE TOO SOON"
NO!
NO!
NOOOO!

MOLLY-- IT'S NOT REAL. IT'S NOT REAL, SWEETIE. YOU'RE OKAY.
HUH?
ARISA?
IT'S OKAY. IT'S JUST THE FEAR. WE MUST BE GETTING CLOSER FOR THAT WAVE TO HIT YOU SO STRONG AND MAKE YOU THINK ABOUT--
--THE TEAM! THEY'RE ALL DEAD! AND I'M RESPONSIBLE, I'M THEIR LEADER! I SHOULD HAVE...
...BUT I DIDN'T... I COULDN'T...
EASY, HONEY. EASY...
IT'S OKAY. IT'S JUST THE FEAR. IT'S ALL IN YOUR MIND. LET IT GO.
JOANN!
I'M GLAD YOU'RE HERE. JUST IN CASE.
I'VE GOT MOLLY'S BACK, BUT I'LL FEEL A WHOLE LOT BETTER KNOWING YOU'VE GOT MINE.
GOOD PLAN, DEAR.
NOW IF WE COULD ONLY FIND--

K-KARL...?
ARE... YOU IN HERE? I CAN'T--
OH!
KARL, IT'S ME. MOLLY.
I CAME TO... I THOUGHT I...UMMM...
SO, WHAT'S GOIN' ON?
S-S-STAY AWAY, MOLLY. I CAN'T CONTROL IT.
I'VE PUSHED EVERYONE AWAY. SCARED THEM.
NO ONE WILL LIKE ME NOW. THEY'LL SEND ME AWAY.
I LIKE YOU, KARL. I'M YOUR FRIEND. AND, LIKE, NO ONE'S GONNA SEND YOU AWAY.
WE ONLY CAME TO HELP 'CAUSE WE'RE YOUR FRIENDS, KARL. MOLLY, ME, JOANN, AND...

...MG?
N-NO...NO--!
THEY'LL SEE! THEY'LL SEE!
IT'S ALL RIGHT, HONEY. RELAX...RELAX.
IS IT OKAY IF WE HELP YOU, KARL? WILL YOU LET US HELP YOU TO CALM DOWN?
TH-THANK YOU, ARISA, BUT I...I THINK I'M ALRIGHT NOW.
WHAT WORRIES ME IS...
...IF HE'S GOING TO BE ALL RIGHT.
NO, NO, NO, NO, NONONONO...

HE'S IN DEEP SHOCK, HONEY. IF WE HAVE ANY HOPE OF GETTING HIM OUT, WE'RE GOING TO HAVE TO GO IN THERE TO GET HIM.
OH, YUCK. JOANN, THIS IS THE ONE PERSON ON THE PLANET THAT I LIKE THE LEAST. ARE YOU SURE THIS ISN'T SOMETHING YOU'D REALLY LIKE TO DO BY YOURSELF?
VERY FUNNY. LET'S GO.
NICE TURN, MERROW-- YOU'RE GETTIN' IT. BUT BE MORE AGGRESSIVE, KID. MILLER, THORNTON--YOU GUYS ARE SUPPOSED TO BE AGENTS, FER CRISSAKE! GET IN SHAPE OR GET OUT! DO FIFTY MORE OF THOSE!
HEY, MOTHY! I SENT YA TO GET MY COFFEE 'BOUT AN HOUR AGO. WHAT, ARE YOUR WINGS BROKE?
N-NO SIR, LIEUTENANT. I'VE GOT IT RIGHT HE--

KREEESH!
WHA--
YOU STUPID, CLUMSY--
AND YOU WONDER WHY YOU'LL NEVER BE AN OPERATIVE?! FIELD AGENTS NEED TO BE SILENT, STEALTHY, AND AGILE, YOU UNCOORDINATED ...KLUTZ!
YOU THINK I WOULD EVER PUT ANY OF MY PEOPLE IN JEOPARDY LIKE THAT?! BY HAVING YOU ON MY TEAM?!
I DON'T KNOW WHY THEY EVEN LET YOU HANG AROUND HERE! YOU DESTROY PRACTICALLY EVERYTHING YOU TOUCH!
S-STOP. STOP IT.
SHUT UP. SHUT--
YOU'RE A JINX, KARL. A TOTAL FAIL--

TYPICAL, "COMPASSIONATE" HAMMERSKOLD.
POOR KARL... NO **WONDER** HE LOST IT.
...URE, NOT A FAILURE, NOT A FAILURE, DAD...
AFTER BEING CAST OUT BY HIS *OWN* PEOPLE, THE **MOTHMEN**, HE'S BEEN **DESPERATE** TO FIT IN HERE AT **BEDLAM**. IT'S BEEN HARD BECAUSE HE *IS* QUITE CLUMSY WITH THOSE **WINGS**. BUT STILL...
NOBODY DESERVES THAT KIND OF ABUSE.
SO, LIKE, HOW IS **HAMMERSKOLD**?
OH, HE SHOULD BE FINE ONCE WE GET HIM **OUT**, BUT IT WILL PROBABLY TAKE A GOOD PART OF THE **NIGHT**. WE COULD USE SOME **PILLOWS** AND A COUPLE POTS OF **COFFEE**.
I'LL GET THEM!
NO!
I'LL GET SOMEONE ELSE TO CARRY THEM.
END

BALLAY,
PHILIPPINES
PROLOGUE

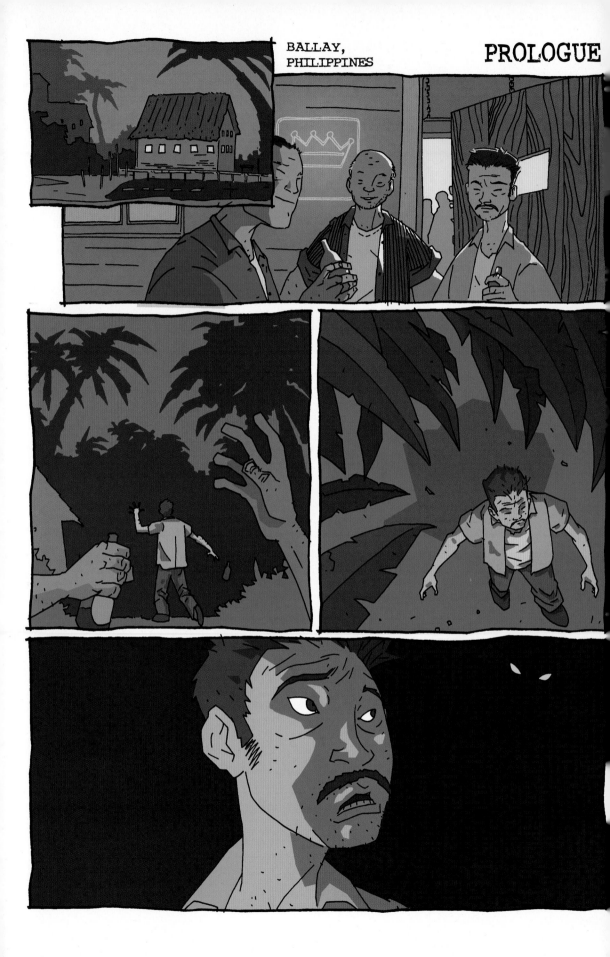

END PROLOGUE

CHAPTER FOUR

C! rico.

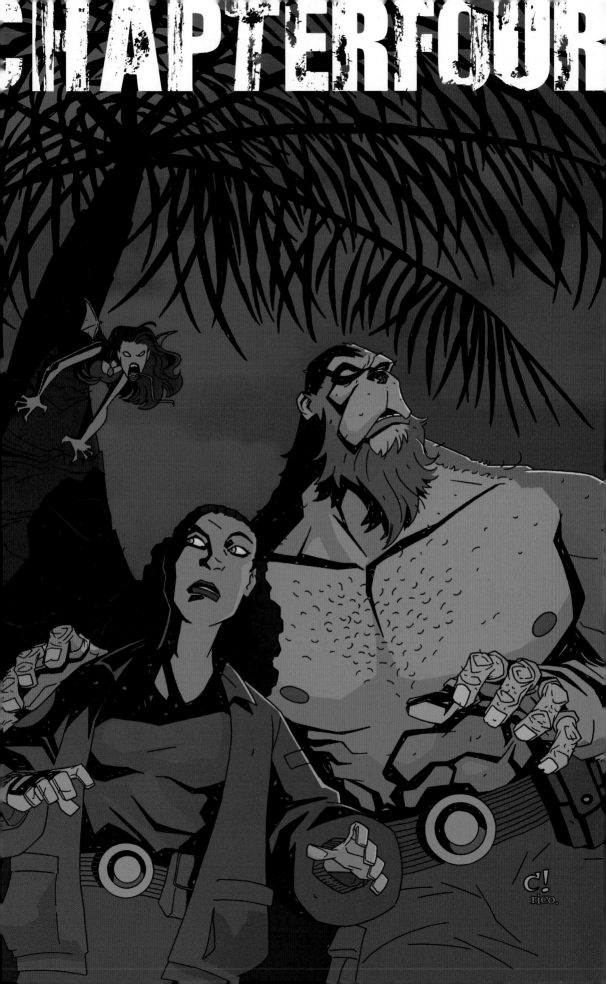

The Chief's office, a short time ago...
CHOOPIE, DO YOU KNOW WHAT OUR NAME, BEDLAM, STANDS FOR?
"NIGHT OF THE ASWANG!"
TODD AND CRAIG'S Perhapanauts in
WORDS-- TODD PICTURES-- CRAIG
COLORS BY RICO
YEAH.
COULD YOU TELL ME?
UMMM...
OH! UHHH...BUREAU OF... EXTRA-DEMOTIONAL-- I MEAN, DIMENSIONAL...
...LIE-UH-BIL-EYE-TIES AND MAN...AGE-MENT.
LIABILITIES.
BEDLAM

AND DO YOU KNOW WHAT THAT WORD **MEANS**? ***"LIABILITY?"***
YEAH.
WHAT DOES IT MEAN?
UMM...
I MEAN, NO.
A LIABILITY IS SOMETHING THAT WE CAN'T BE ***CERTAIN*** OF, SOMETHING THAT COULD GO ***WRONG.***
YOU, CHOOPIE... ARE A LIABILITY.
AS WE SAW WITH THE ***CHIMAERA*** THE OTHER DAY...YOU TOOK IT UPON ***YOURSELF*** TO...***CLOSE*** THE D-GATE BEFORE THE CHIMAERA WAS COMPLETELY THROUGH...

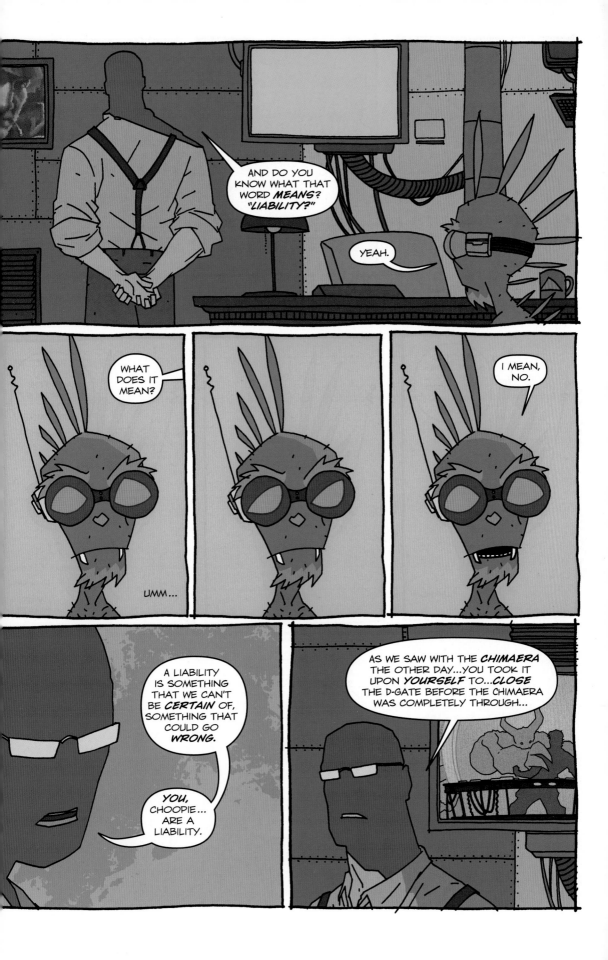

...DO YOU REMEMBER THAT?
UH-HUH.
YOU CUT IT IN HALF...
UH-HUH.
...WHICH KILLED IT.
UH-HUH.
WHICH IS SOMETHING WE TRY TO AVOID AROUND HERE.
UH-HUH.
WHAT DID YOU HAVE FOR BREAKFAST THIS MORNING?
UH-HUH.
WAIT. WHAT?
WHAT I'M SAYING, CHOOPIE, IS THAT WE CAN'T AFFORD ANY LIABILITIES HERE AT BEDLAM. IF YOU WANT TO STAY ON ARISA'S TEAM, WE NEED TO SEE SOME IMPROVEMENT.
YOU NEED TO START THINKING BEFORE YOU ACT. I WON'T TOLERATE ANY MORE OF THESE "ACCIDENTS." ONE MORE, AND YOU'LL BE TAKEN OFF ACTIVE DUTY--
--INDEFINITELY.
HAVE I MADE MYSELF CLEAR?
...
UH-HUH.

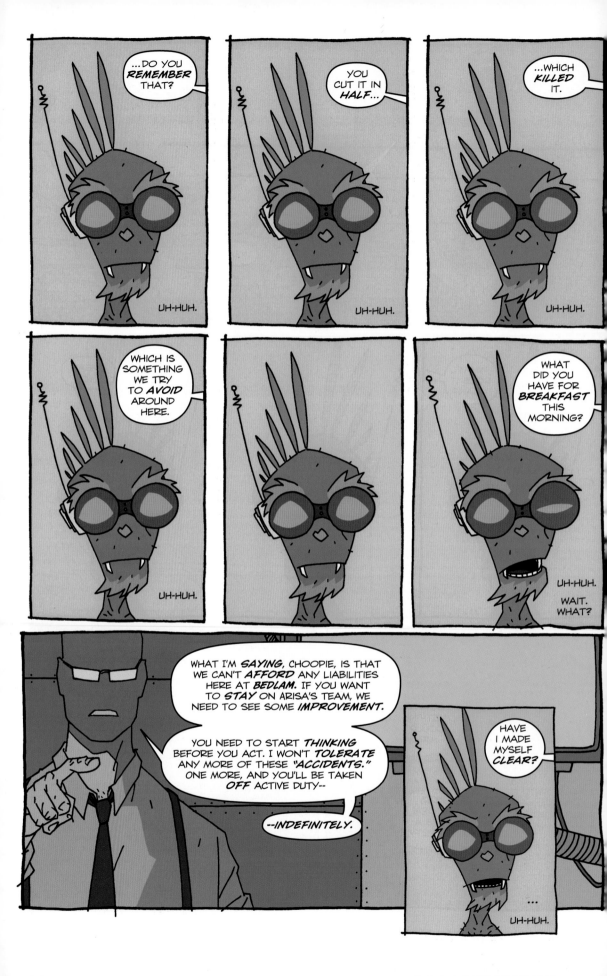

RAZZA FRAZZIN' SUMMA LIABILITY...
FRINK FRANK RAZZA FRAZZIN' ACCIDENT...
...YOU HAVE A RAZZA FRAZZIN' ACCIDENT!
fwink!
Click
Click-Clack
Click
Click
Click
...CALL ME RAZZA FRAZZIN' LIABILITY. YOU'RE--
Clack
HUH?!

WHAT THE--?
HMM?
Whrr
Whrrrr
no smoking
FWASH!
GAH!
WHA--? OH, NO YOU DON'T!
COME BACK HERE!
Clack
Clack
I SAID COME BACK HERE! YER NOT GETTIN' AWAY FROM--
UH!
fwink!
BONK!

WHAT THE FREAK WAS *THAT...?*
THERE HE IS!
CHOOPIE, WHERE'VE YOU *BEEN?* LET'S *GO!* WE'RE LEAVING IN, LIKE, A *MINUTE!*
HUH? WHERE WE GOIN'?
THE PHILIPPINES.
WHAT'S IN THE PHILIPPINES?
THAT'S WHAT WE'RE GOING TO FIND OUT.
BIG...?

THERE'VE BEEN SOME ATTACKS IN THE VILLAGE OF BALLAY THE LOCAL POLICE ARE CALLING UNRELATED, BUT...
...I HAVE A THEORY THEY'RE SOMETHING ELSE.
"FILIPINO LEGEND TELLS OF A CREATURE CALLED THE ASWANG.
A TERRIFYING AND BRUTAL PREDATOR, BY DAY IT IS SAID TO TAKE ON THE ASPECT OF A COMMON MONGREL.
"AT NIGHT, HOWEVER, IT CAN TRANSFORM ITSELF INTO A BEAUTIFUL--AND MESMERIZING--WOMAN.
"ONCE IT LOCATES IT'S PREY, THE ASWANG SEPARATES ITSELF FROM IT'S LOWER TORSO--
"--ROOSTING ON ROOFTOPS AND AMID SHADOWED TREE BRANCHES, POISED TO DESCEND UPON IT'S VICTIM AND EXTRACT EVERY DROP OF BLOOD WITH IT'S LONG, STRAW-LIKE TONGUE."
STINKIN' VAMPIRES!

THIS IS A VICIOUS, CUNNING CREATURE, GANG, CAPABLE OF SOME HORRIFIC VIOLENCE. WE NEED TO STAY CAREFUL.
BLOOD-SUCKING FREAK!
Y'KNOW, CHOOPIE...
UM...
NAH.
NEVERMIND.
THE WHOLE PLACE IS, LIKE, DESERTED.
THERE'RE NO LIGHTS ON... AND IT LOOKS LIKE SOME WINDOWS ARE ACTUALLY BOARDED UP!
WELL, DESPITE WHAT THE LOCAL POLICE MIGHT SAY, I'M SURE THAT THESE PEOPLE CAN SENSE THAT THERE'S SOMETHING...EVIL STALKING THEIR VILLAGE.

'KAY, EVERYBODY-- LET'S SPREAD OUT AND STAY OUT OF SIGHT. AND LIKE BIG SAID, BE CAREFUL. I'M GONNA LINK US UP TELEPATHICALLY--WHICH IS WHY WE LEFT THE HEADSETS HOME-- BUT THAT DOESN'T MEAN DON'T REPORT IN REGULARLY. LET'S LET EACH OTHER KNOW WHERE WE ARE AND WHAT WE SEE. 'KAY?
and soon--
ANYTHING, MG?
NOTHING, ARISA. I'VE SET MY 'CATOR TO DETECT MOTION, SINCE IT WASN'T PICKING UP ANYTHING ON ANY OF THE OTHER SPECTRUMS. BUT I STILL--
WHOA. WAIT A MINUTE...

NO. I THOUGHT I HAD SOMETHING, BUT IT STO--
SKRRRIP!
UNHH!
MG!
NO!
UNNH--
THUNK
MOLLY! CHOOPIE! GO HIGH! SEE IF YOU CAN SPOT THAT THING!
BIG! GET TO MG! GET HIM BACK TO THE SKIP AND SEE WHAT YOU CAN DO!

WHAT--? WAS THAT CHOOPIE OR--
CHOOPIE, WHERE ARE YOU?
JUST ABOVE THE CHURCH THINGY.
THEN IT WAS HER.
THERE.
OKAY--LET'S SEE HOW THIS BITCH LIKES A PSYCHIC BLADE RIGHT BETWEEN THE--
THERE SHE IS-- JUST HOVERING AGAINST THE CEILING, WAITING FOR ME TO--
NO!
IT'S A MIRROR! SHE--

AAARHHHHH!
SKKRRRRRRIPP!
AAARHHHHH!
ARISA?
ARISA, WHERE ARE YOU?!
ARISA?!
BIG, SHE'S HURT! WHAT DO WE--

SKKRASSSCH!
UNT--
--
smack smack
HUH?
BIG...?
ARISA...?

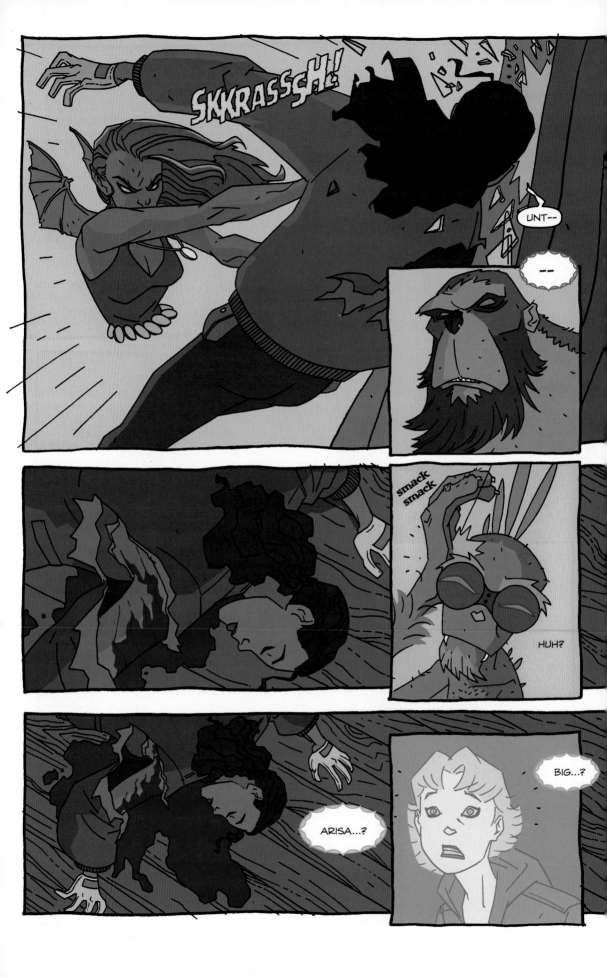

"ARISA?!"

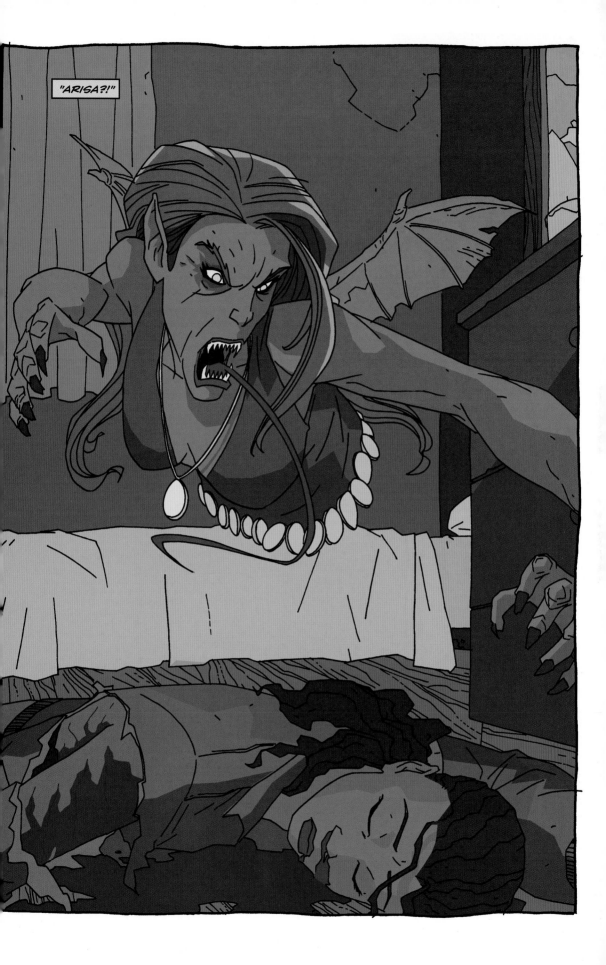

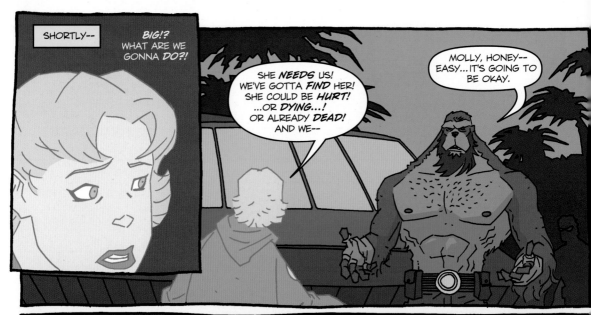

SHORTLY--

BIG!? WHAT ARE WE GONNA *DO?!*

SHE *NEEDS* US! WE'VE GOTTA *FIND* HER! SHE COULD BE *HURT!* ...OR *DYING...!* OR ALREADY *DEAD!* AND WE--

MOLLY, HONEY-- EASY...IT'S GOING TO BE OKAY.

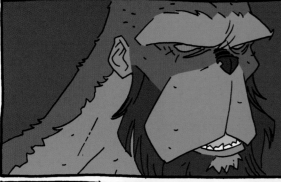

CHOOPIE'S STILL OUT THERE. AND WHILE I WOULD HAVE *PREFERRED* HE CHECK IN AS *YOU* DID, I THINK HE'S OUR BEST BET. HE HAS A BETTER CHANCE OF FINDING ARISA THAN ANY OF US. HIS NOSE AND HUNTING INSTINCTS ARE STILL QUITE SHARP.

UNFORTUNATELY, WHEN WE DECIDED TO RELY ON ARISA'S *TELEPATHY* TO KEEP US LINKED, WE NEGLECTED TO CONSIDER THAT THE HEADSETS ALSO HOUSE OUR *LOCATOR* ELEMENTS. WE HAVE NO WAY OF *TRACKING* ARISA.

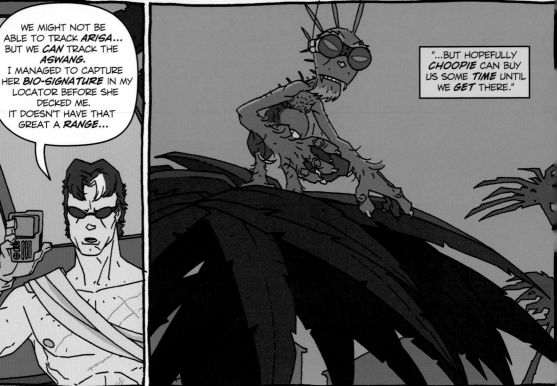

WE MIGHT NOT BE ABLE TO TRACK *ARISA...* BUT WE *CAN* TRACK THE *ASWANG.* I MANAGED TO CAPTURE HER *BIO-SIGNATURE* IN MY LOCATOR BEFORE SHE DECKED ME. IT DOESN'T HAVE THAT GREAT A *RANGE...*

"...BUT HOPEFULLY *CHOOPIE* CAN BUY US SOME *TIME* UNTIL WE *GET* THERE."

SNIFF
SNIFF
GOTTA DO THIS...
GOTTA SHOW 'EM.
GOTTA FIND
ARISA...
NOT A LIARBILITY...
DOWN THERE...
HER SCENT...
AND...
BLOOD...
ARISA!
NO!

CRACK!
I SMELLED YOU WERE HERE, LITTLE BLOOD-DRINKER...
...I COULD NOT BELIEVE MY NOSE, BUT IT WAS TRUE!
UCK!
THEY HAVE MADE YOU INTO ONE OF THEM! A PITIABLE PET!
THEY HAVE TAKEN AWAY YOUR NATURE, YOUR FEROCITY, YOUR ESSENCE.
I CAN TELL YOU DON'T HUNT ANYMORE. YOU DON'T HUNGER. YOU DON'T KILL.
THEY PACKAGE UP YOUR BLOOD-MEAL AND SEND YOU ON YOUR WAY. THEY TREAT YOU AS A CHILD, A SERVANT, A COMMON DOG...
...AND YOU ACCEPT IT.
BUT SMELL THAT BLOOD, CHUPAS. SMELL THE COPPERY LIFE.
YOU CAN ALMOST TASTE IT, CAN'T YOU? METALLIC AND RICH ON YOUR TONGUE.
IT'S BEEN SO LONG SINCE YOU DRANK FRESH.
WARM.

GO AHEAD. JUST ONE SMALL TASTE. IT CAN'T HURT. TO FEEL IT TRICKLE DOWN YOUR THROAT. SO WARM.
NO.
TO FEEL HER PULSE PUMPING IT INTO YOUR MOUTH.
REMEMBER?
NO.
YOU WANT IT. GO AHEAD.
JUST ONE SMALL TASTE.
NO ONE WILL KNOW.
NO.
TELL THEM IT WAS ME.
NO.

I'LL BE FINE. I'M NOT GOING TO JUST LAY AROUND WHILE ARISA'S IN TROUBLE.
THE WOUND WAS DEEP.
I CLEANED IT OUT AS BEST I COULD. THERE...
...THERE WASN'T MUCH BLOOD.
UHH...
...GOOD?
THIS IS IT. THE BIO-SIGNATURE MATCHES PERFECTLY. IT'S GOTTA BE HER.
READY?
AHHH!
!
MG--SHOOT IT! SHOOT IT!
I CAN'T! I MIGHT HIT BIG!
UH! UH!
kick
kick
kick

NO! I DON'T WANNA DO THIS.
BUT, I... IT WOULD TASTE SO... GOOOOOD...
AND NO ONE WOULD KNOW... IF I...
JUST...
ONE...
LITTLE...
NO!
I'M NOT THAT ANYMORE.
I'M...
ARISA'S MY TEAMMATE, MY...SISTER--
--MY FRIEND!

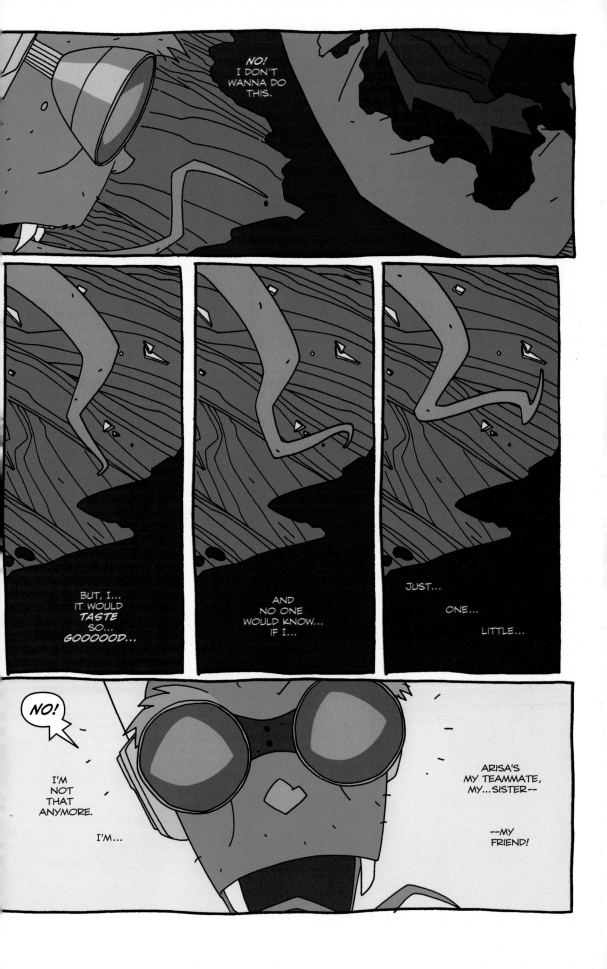

C'MON, ARISA! WAKE UP! WAKE UP!
HEY! HEY, YOU GUYS!
OVER HERE!
HELP!
THAT WAY! IT'S CHOOPIE!
CHOOPIE!
OMIGOD--
--ARISA!!
SHE'S LOST A LOT OF BLOOD. WE'LL HAVE TO GET HER TO THE MED-LAB AS FAST AS WE CAN.
I'VE FOUND A COUPLE OF EXTRA WORMHOLES, MOLLY. WE'LL BE THERE IN ABOUT THREE MINUTES.

)SHRAK CRACKLE(...DENY THAT REQUEST, BLUE TEAM! REPEAT--YOU ARE NOT CLEARED FOR REENTRY! TAKE IT SOMEWHERE ELSE. WE...WE'VE GOT A... A SITUATION DOWN HERE.
WHAT KIND OF SITUATION, BASE?
LET'S JUST SAY, BLUE, THAT SOMEONE OPENED THE WRONG D-GATE!
CONTINUED...?

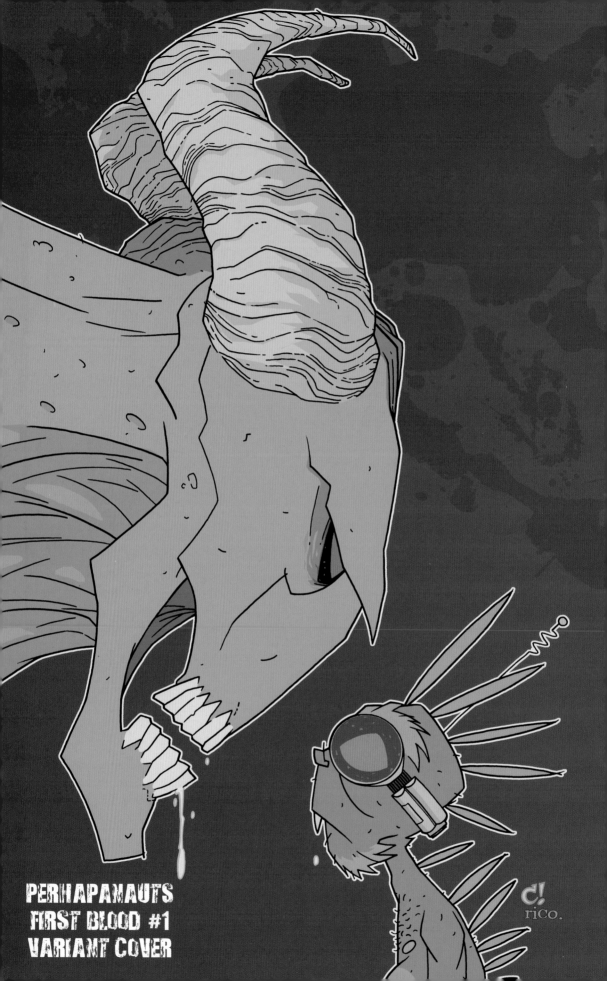

PERHAPANAUTS
FIRST BLOOD #1
VARIANT COVER

⇒KRRKK⇐ -IN, BLUE TEAM! COME IN! WE LOST ⇒KRRRKLK⇐ -IGNAL!
BOOM
⇒KRRR⇐ ARISA...?
⇒KRRRK⇐ REPORT! STERIS? MONJO...?
IT...IT WAS A SET-UP, CHIEF! THEY KNEW WE WERE COMING! WE WERE AMBUSHED AS SOON AS WE HIT THE DECK! THERE WERE SLEEPERS EVERYWHERE!!
BOOM
I... I THINK...
I THINK EVERYONE ELSE IS DEAD...
BOOM
BOOOMM
SEVEN MONTHS EARLIER
by
TODD AND CRAIG 2K3
colors -RICO 2K6
THE 'CATOR'S FRIED--
--I'M NOT GETTING ANY MAPS OR ANYTHING. I'M GONNA HAFTA USE MY HEAD TO FIND THE TARGET...
AND HOPE THAT I CAN "FEEL" HIM THROUGH THE DAMPENERS...
SECURITY! AND THEY'RE LOOKING FOR ME, NO DOUBT.
I'LL WAIT FOR THE NEXT EXPLOSION--

BOOOOMM
-- AND USE IT TO HOPEFULLY COVER MY DASH!
THERE SHE IS! FIRE!!
ZIMM
ZIM
ZIMM
OR NOT.
LEAST THAT LAST BLAST BLOCKED THEIR WAY FROM FOLLOWING ME.
UNFORTUNATELY, MY "SCAN'S" BEING BLOCKED AS WELL. THEY'VE GOT DAMPENERS ALL OVER THIS PLACE--
BUT MAYBE THAT'S JUST THE CLUE I NEED. JUST LOOK FOR THE ROOM WITH THE MOST--
BINGO!! THAT'S GOTTA BE WHERE THEY'VE GOT HIM...
KRRKK RISA. WE'VE GOT A CHKKK WHAT'S YOUR "TWENTY"? WE KSSHHK-

HOLD UP WITH THE QUESTIONS RIGHT NOW, BASE.
ACCESS PANEL'S ENGULFED, BUT MAYBE I CAN STILL GET THROUGH --
pop
SPIKT
"--WITH A LITTLE SNOT*."
*SENTIENT NANO-ORGANISM TECHNOLOGY
SSSSHHHHUUUPP
SSSSHHHHUUUPP
CHIEF--
I'M IN.
TARGET ACQUIRED.
huhh? whoo...
MY NAME'S ARISA.
I'M WITH THE GOOD GUYS.
I'M HERE TO GET YOU OUT.

⊰CHHHK⊱ PROCEED WITH OBJECTIVE, ⊰KRK⊱ -RISA... CAN YOU ⊰KRRK⊱
CAN YOU... 'SENSE'... IF ANY OTHER ⊰KRK⊱ -LUE TEAM SURVIVED?
N-NO, CHIEF, I...
CHOOP DID HIS THING AND GOT OUT BEFORE WE GOT HERE. THE ONLY OTHER BLUE I CAN "FEEL" IS--
--MOLLY? ARE YOU THERE?
I'M ON LEVEL THREE, 'RIS... STANDING JUST BELOW THE TACHYON ACCELERATOR...
CHUM CHUM CHUM CHUM CHUM
THE WHOLE PLACE IS COMING DOWN AROUND US, MOL. TAKE THAT THING OUT AS FAST AS YOU CAN AND EVAC! THERE'S NO WAY WE CAN LET THEM--
NO, 'RIS... IT'S WORSE THAN THAT...
...IT'S BEEN PRIMED.
PRIMED?!
MOLLY, GET OUT OF HERE! ABORT MISSION, JUST--
FREEZE! HOLD IT RIGHT THERE!
SLEEPERS! DAMN.
FREEZE! HOLD IT RIGHT THERE!
crap.

THAT DOOR THERE. QUICK, I'M RIGHT BEHIND YOU...
...GO!
uh-kay. uh-kay.
uh... HI, GUYS! I WAS JUST WONDERING... DO YOU HAVE A LADIES ROOM AROUND HE--
JUST SHUT UP! WE'RE--
OMIGOD! WHAT'S SHE--?! I ... I CAN SEE RIGHT--
I SAID FREEZ--
UNNGH!
SORRY, FOR THE PSYCHIC K.O., BOYS--
--BUT THE CLOCK IS TICKING!
NUHHN!
whoa! it's not...
we can'd go dis way...
we're up... there's no...
BOOM
BOOM
I KNOW! JUST GO! JUST--
UNGFF!
NO...

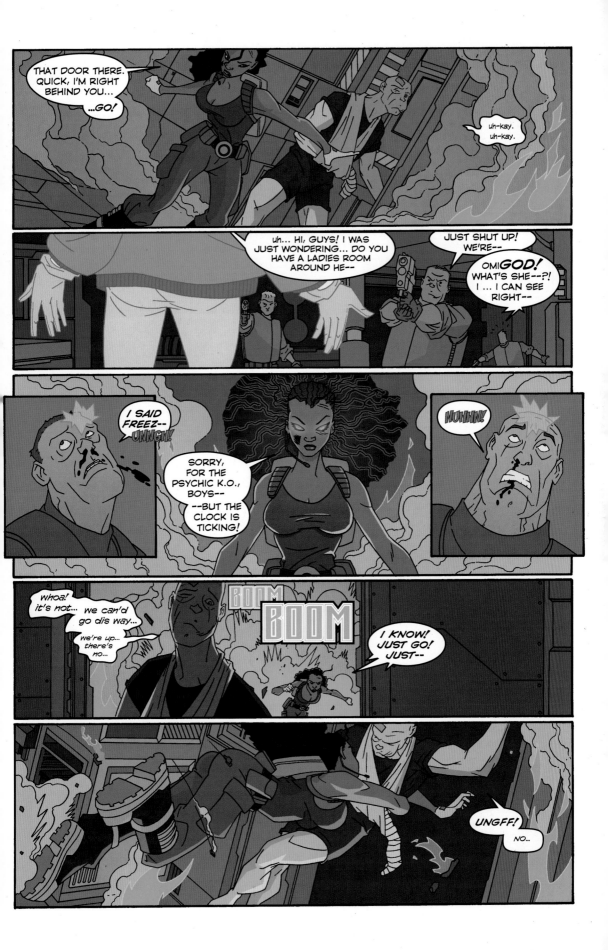

NO! DON'T SHOOT! YOU MIGHT HIT THE--
ZIMM
ZIM
ZIMM
MOLLY? WHERE ARE YA, MOL?
GET OUT, ARISA! GO! IT'S TOO LATE! THEY SHOT THE--
BOOM
BOOM

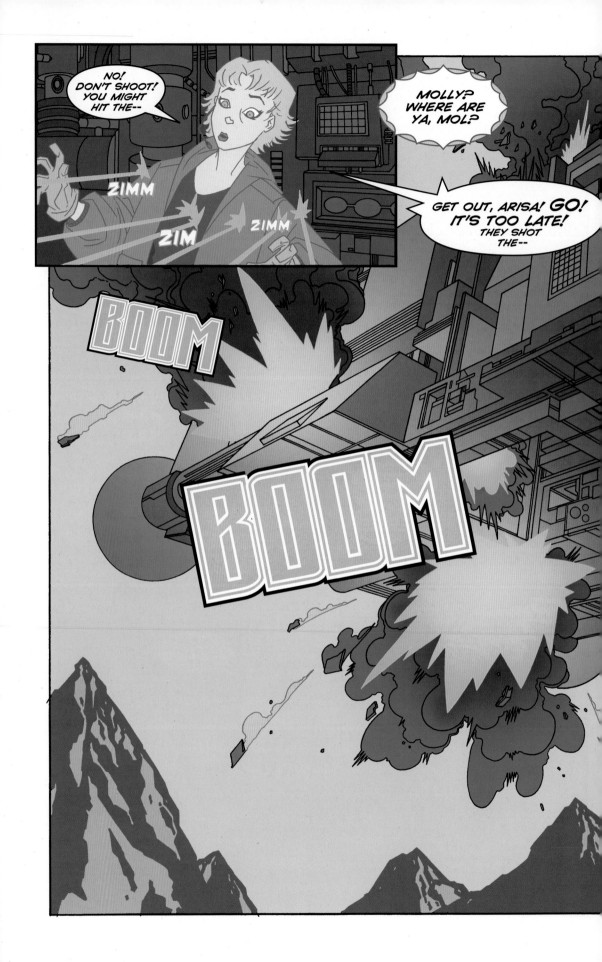

NO!! MOLLY, GET OUT! YOU DON'T KNOW IF YOU'LL--
MOLLY?
BOOOMM
MOLLY!
bye, 'ris.
SHOOOMM

MOLLY!!
NO.
...
MOLLY...
PLEASE... TELL ME THAT'S... A PARACHUTE YOU'RE WEARING...
IT'S A PARACHUTE, RIGHT...?
...RIGHT?
SNF
...
IT'S NOT A PARACHUTE.
ENGAGE.
TUP
ARISA? KRRRK... UR STATUS? CHK
ARISA? CHK
ARISA?

THE BEGINNING...

WELL, INITIALLY I WAS JUST GOING TO RECALIBRATE THE MODGING, BUT THEN I THOUGHT I'D BETTER DE-SALITATE THE FIEPICK FIRST OR THAT BILLING'S PROVULATOR IS GOING TO FROG UP.
YOU DON'T WANT THAT.
HI, YOU GUYS...
FIEPICK
BY TODD AND CRAIG 2K3
COLORS - RICO 2K6

...UH... CAN I HELP?
...
I DON'T KNOW, CHOOPIE--
--CAN YOU HELP?
BLINK
BLINK
I MEAN, DO YOU KNOW ANYTHING ABOUT ANY OF THIS STUFF?
OF COURSE I DO. I KNOW 'BOUT LOTSA STUFF! I KNOW 'BOUT THE MODGING... THINGY. AND THE SALIVATOR. AND THE BILL'S OVULATOR.
BLINK
BLINK

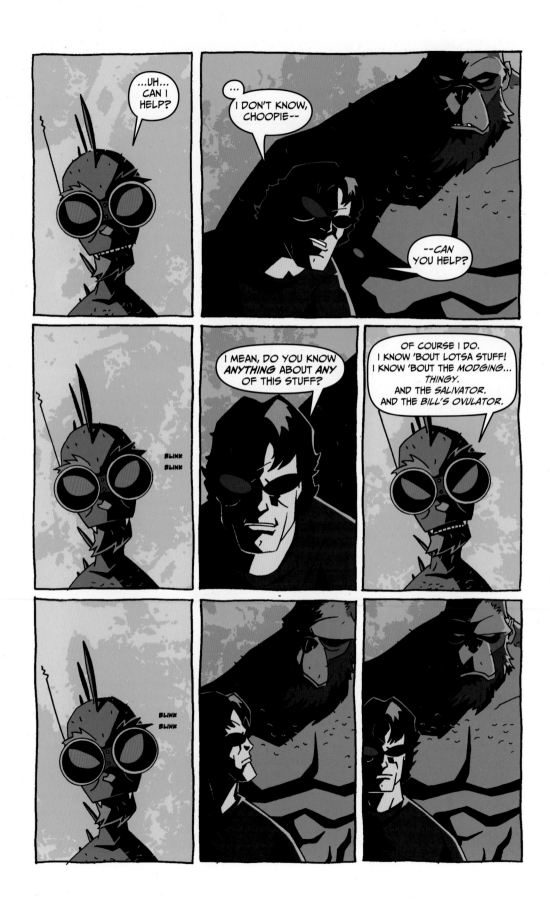

I KNOW 'BOUT THE FIEPICK!!
REALLY?
YUP.
YOU'RE SURE?
YOU BETCHA!
YOU REALLY KNOW WHICH ONE THE FIEPICK IS?
YES, MISTER SMARTY. I DID READ SOME OF THE MANUALS THEY MADE US STUDY FOR BLUE TEAM.
CHOOPIE, COULD YOU HAND ME THE FIEPICK?
COULD I...
UHHH...

UNLESS MAYBE YOU... FORGOT WHICH ONE IS...
NO, NO I REMEMBER...
...IT'S, UMMM...
...LEMME SEE...
'CAUSE I CAN UNDERSTAND HOW THAT FIEPICK MIGHT BE HARD TO REMEMBER...
HEH.
WHAT'S THAT, MOLLY? WOULD I LIKE SOME WHAT...?!?
PIE?!!
I LOVE PIE!!
SORRY, GUYS-- I CAN'T HELP YA ANYMORE! I GOTTA GO!
PIE!
end.

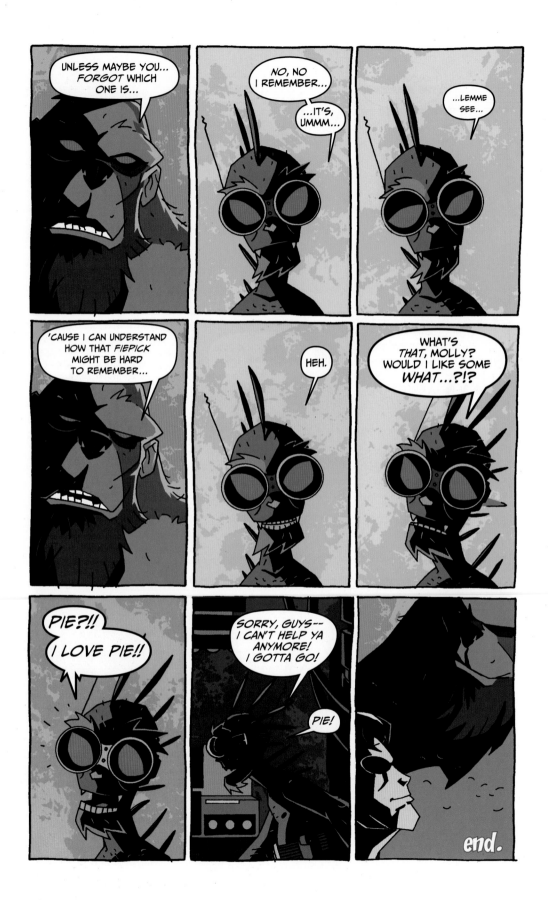

BEDLAM FILES
ARISA HINES

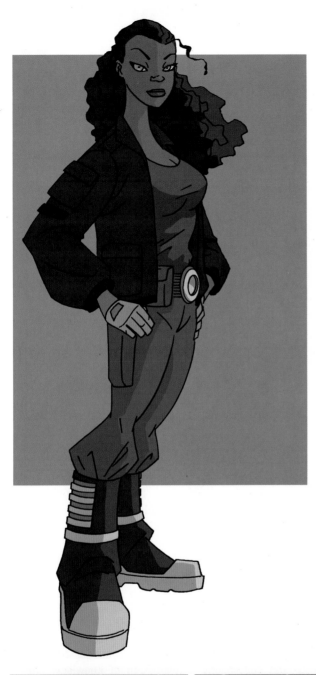

Arisa came to BEDLAM all of three years ago, led here, uncannily, by her various psychic talents. (She is possessed of strong telepathic and telekinetic skills and an as-yet undefined level of prescience.) She was initially brought into Red Group as a neophyte during the rigorous training each team member undergoes, but soon found herself recruited into Blue Group when need arose for someone with her unique abilities. Unfortunately, her second outing with that Team left her the sole survivor of an horrific ambush, a young girl of 19, terrified yet determined to fulfill the mission's objective on her own. Which she accomplished admirably.

She has become both friend and disciple to Joann DeFile, our Psychic and Spiritual Guide (see file: DeFile, Joann 92/3-2), whose role as mentor and advisor I trust implicitly. Arisa's strength and resourcefulness have made me certain that she was the best choice to lead the newly reformed Blue Group. Her reluctance and vociferous objections to this new role only serve to reinforce my decision. She is a strong leader whose only fault may lie in the fact that she cares about the members of her team too much.

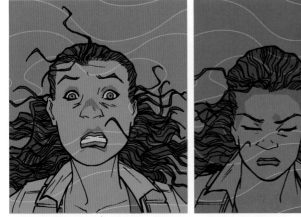
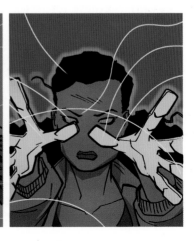

BEDLAM FILES

BIG

a.k.a SASQUATCH
a.k.a YETI
a.k.a. BIGFOOT

"BIG" has been at BEDLAM actually since before there was a BEDLAM.

Captured in 1973 in the Northern Corridor section of British Columbia, Big was captured and held for several years by Project Entua, a clandestine government program designed to retrieve and study cryptozoological specimens from around the world.

When BEDLAM was formed, it was Drs. Alazar and Das (see files: Alazar, Antonio, PhD – Das, Baldev MD FAAP) who petitioned for the Sasquatch to be brought here and soon was the first subject to undergo Alazar's rudimentary Evolvo-Ray.

An already strong creature, Big was soon displaying feats of immeasurable strength and dexterity. But it was the incredible emergence of intelligence and subsequent accumulation of knowledge that astounded the Doctors and BEDLAM Staff alike. Not long after, Big was a colleague rather than subject and soon was working side-by-side with the Doctors to perfect the very Evolvo-Ray that brought him into the future. His intelligence quotient ratings exceed the scale and his ability to comprehend grossly abstract theories (and realities) is, to me, astounding to experience.

Recently, for reasons of his own (my guess is that he wishes to both supervise Choopie and work closely with our newest acquisition, MG), Big has accepted Arisa's invitation to join Blue Team. He has always proven to be both a resourceful and effective agent and his presence on the team, I'll admit, has me resting much easier as well.

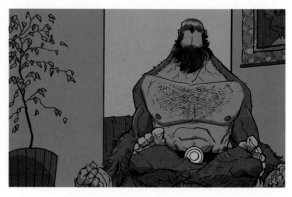

BEDLAM FILES
CHOOPIE
a.k.a Chupacabra

"Choopie", as he has been so labelled...named, was detected and apprehended by Red Team in the Spring of 1996. A vicious and voracious predator, he was one of a suspected group of such creatures creating a flap of sightings in the suburbs of Puerto Rico at that time. (How these creatures originally gained egress to our realm from their own still remains a mystery as the dimensional integrity was violently rent rather than weakened via natural entropic means.)

The creature was captured while attempting to wrest a kitten it had pursued from the manifold of a 1987 Honda Civic. Choopie was studied for several days by BEDLAM's BioLogic Department, but was soon exposed to Dr. Alazar's Evolvo-Ray at the request of Big. The treatment resulted in a creature with a personality very much like that of a 6 year old boy. Though his phenomenal speed, agility, and ability to fly make him a potentially invaluable agent, Choopie is, in my opinion, erratic and unreliable, and often is the cause of much damage within the BEDLAM facility. He is, I'm told, quite fond of, and loyal to, Arisa and the rest of her team and so carries out assignments and missions with the best of intentions.

BEDLAM FILES
PETER HAMMERSKOLD

Peter Hammerskold, it should be noted, is a soldier first, a telepsychometrist second. Exhibiting the gift of telepsychometry as a teen, Peter was a second lieutenant in the US Marine Corps when we 'acquired' him to become an agent for BEDLAM. Sadly, he was never quite able to leave his military inclinations behind.

Hammerskold has been a member of Red Team for almost five years now, Leader of that Group for two. He is an extremely efficient strategist and is gradually becoming more and more adapt at dealing with the inexplicable and the unknown. He uses a firm hand with his Team, but not to the point of cruelty or insensitivity. He cares for them but is reluctant to let that show. He is a good man.

Regrettably, however, Hammerskold carries a deep-seated bitterness regarding his continued placement in Red Team, believing, somehow, that Blue Group is the 'premiere' team. He has petitioned me repeatedly to be given command of Blue Team, feeling that the group would be much more effective in his charge. That I chose to appoint Arisa as Team Leader has only exacerbated Hammerskold's frustration in this matter.

Though he works well and conducts himself in a professional manner when Team missions coincide, his resentment is obvious. He is ever confrontational when dealing with Arisa and criticizes her every move.

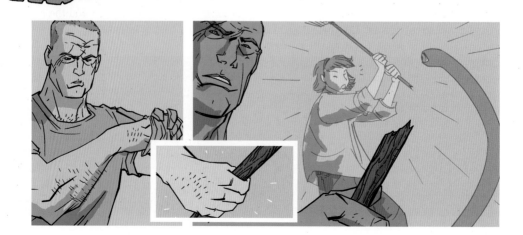

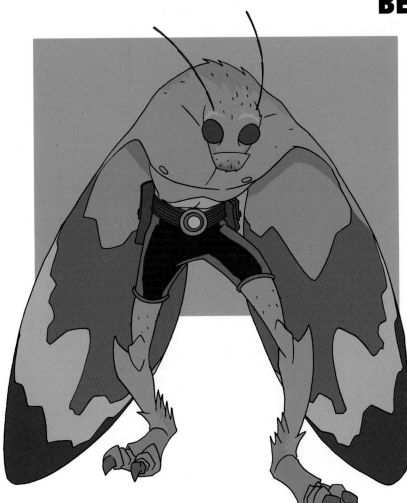

BEDLAM FILES
MOTHMAN
a.k.a Karl

Poor Karl. Relegated to the role of Reservist, it would seem that, while Karl aspires to become a full time member of Blue Team, he will, sadly, never make it higher than on call, a perhapanaut-in-waiting.

Karl is a Mothman (see files: Mothman 79/8; Keel, John 68/7-12), a race or tribe of enigmatic beings whose nature and motivations remain a mystery to us here at Bedlam. Hinted at through history as harbingers of doom and destruction, these dark "angels of death" have been sighted days and sometimes weeks prior to major disasters, (the most reported contemporary case taking place in 1968 in the Ohio River valley near Point Pleasant, West Virginia). What is known of these creatures is that they are (highly?) sentient, can travel temporally, and are capable of projecting an aura of absolute terror (possibly hypnotic in nature...?). What we do know about them comes as a result of investigation and what limited information we have been able to glean from Karl. He is reluctant to divulge information regarding his brethren or their practices.

Unfortunately, Karl's situation was actually predicated by agents of Bedlam. In our attempt to make contact with these strange and eerie creatures, Karl was...detained and studied. He was unresponsive and refused to even acknowledge his situation. Upon his release, however, he was shunned by his caste and banished from their group as an outcast. With nowhere else to turn, Karl eventually ended up here, though understandably averse to betraying his people in any way.

Also unfortunate is Karl's desire to please and his (unrealistic) dreams of being an full time agent on one of our teams. Though he is called in from time to time to assist using his considerable abilities, his large wings and lack of hands or opposable digits, makes him awkward and ineffective as a covert agent. His clumsiness continues to be his personal albatross and, though his intentions are always the best, his mere presence on a mission could potentially jeopardize the case and all involved.

BEDLAM FILES
MERROW

The water-nymph of Irish lore, the dancing, shimmering sprite, the Merrow is a water elemental, the flash of streaking silver glimpsed just below the surface of sunlit streams and glimmering brooks. She remains an agent of Bedlam (Red Team) mostly because she is fascinated (almost consumed) by the ways (and motivations) of mankind.

She is of the mysterious, elusive faerie and relates to others (human and non-human alike) in an empathic manner rather than one of social necessity. (She is drawn–or repelled–to an individual's aurally projected personae and not their sometimes superficial countenance.). She is a quietly curious creature, pure and honest in her thoughts, emotions, reactions. She is sometimes difficult to 'read' as her reactions to both positive and negative information or stimuli evoke the same 'curious' response.

In that the Merrow is practically 'one with the water' once she makes contact, she is a great asset to the team as well as a sort of living personality tester when presented/confronted with new personel. She is, surprisingly, very fond (once again, fascinated) of her Team Leader, Peter Hammerskold

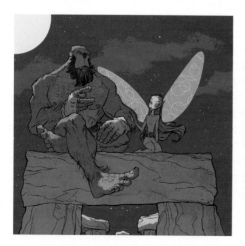 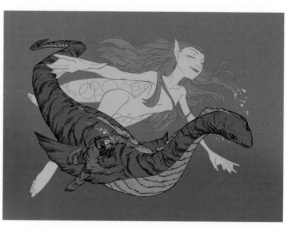

BEDLAM FILES
MG
real name UNKNOWN

With us for only seven months, MG remains a mystery. Refusing to undergo any physical or intellectual testing, he continues to work and reside at BEDLAM as long as we honor his request that we not attempt to investigate either his physiognomy or his past.

He possesses an impressive understanding of machines, intra- and extra-dimensional phenomenon, and the unknown. More importantly, he is able to personally traverse the dimensional barriers or boundaries, and detect their closeness and weak points. This is a gift that he can only affect upon himself.

He possesses an impressive understanding of machines, intra- and extra-dimensional phenomenon, and the unknown. More importantly, he is able to personally traverse the dimensional barriers or boundaries, and detect their closeness and weak points. This is a gift that he can only affect upon himself.

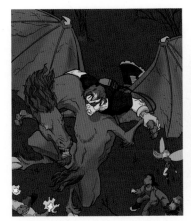

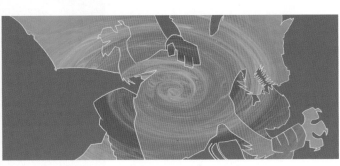

BEDLAM FILES
MOLLY MacALLISTAR

In the records, we classify Molly as a revenant, though it's much easier to simply think of her as a ghost. That Molly herself takes issue with any such terminology–refusing to even discuss the subject– is only the tip of the iceberg here. She came to us, or rather, was located by a new apparatus developed in the ectolabs of r&d, nearly seven years ago. Newly... liberated of her mortal coil, Molly was lost and afraid and, sadly, unaware of her new condition. Contacted and befriended by our resident psychic, Joann DeFile, Molly soon felt herself at home here at BEDLAM and eventually agreed to undergo counseling with Dr. Sheehan (see file: Sheehan, M Patricia, MSW, CSW 67/8-10), which greatly helped Molly to deal with her new situation and surroundings.

She has become both friend and disciple to Joann DeFile, our Psychic and Spiritual Guide (see file: DeFile, Joann 92/3-2), whose role as mentor and advisor I trust implicitly. Arisa's strength and resourcefulness have made me certain that she was the best choice to lead the newly reformed Blue Group. Her reluctance and vociferous objections to this new role only serve to reinforce my decision. She is a strong leader whose only fault may lie in the fact that she cares about the members of her team too much.

It is believed that Molly is more a 'half-ghost', as, while she cannot completely pass into the 'next world', she appears to be rooted here, to this plane of existence, by some lot or some manner of unfinished business. She can regulate her own visibility.

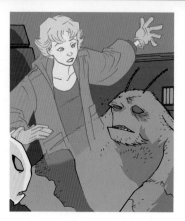

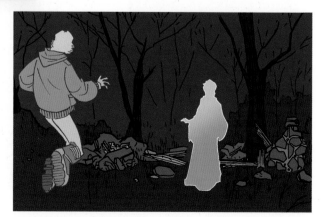

SECOND CHANCES
CHAPTER ONE

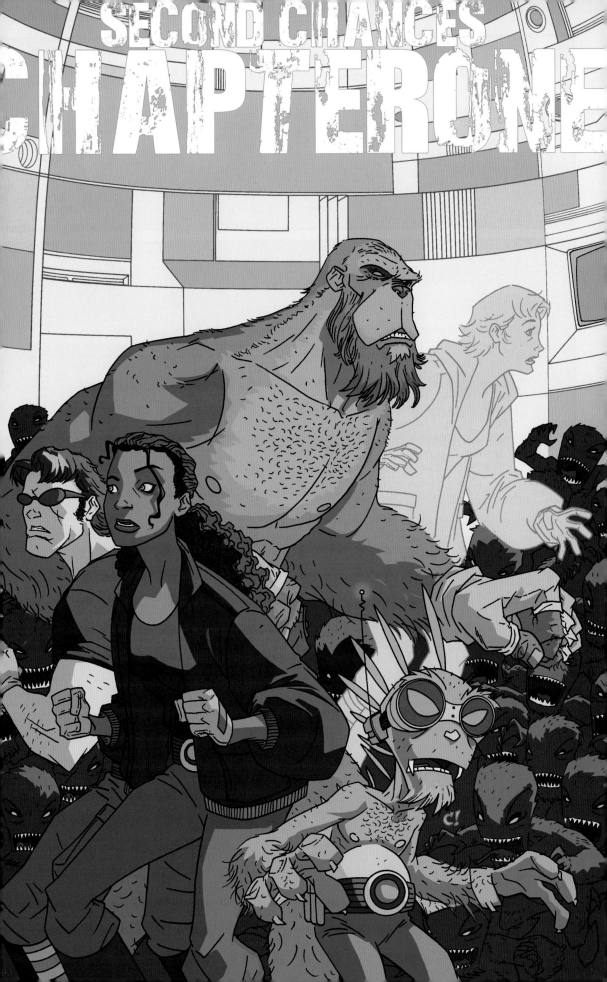

D-GATE: PLATFORM 2
)KRRACKLE(SCORES OF 'EM SWARMING)SKRACKLE(-NTIRE THEATER!
)KRRK(REPEAT: SKORM SWARMING-
BIONEERING
-INFILTRATING ENTIRE COMPLEX. LEVELS 2 AND 3 COMPROMISED. LEVEL 4; BIONEERING, BIOLOGICS, BOTASH...
THE
TODD AND CRAIG'S
Perhapanauts
IN
"TOO BIG!"
TODD--WORDS
CRAIG--PICTURES
RICO--COLORS
ADMIN 4: OFFICE OF DIRECTOR
...TOTAL LOCKDOWN. INITIATE ANDROMEDA PROTOCOLS.
QUARTERS: RED
OH, MY--OMIGOD. IT'S THEM. THEY'RE EVERYWHERE.

WHAT DO YOU MEAN, "THEM"? WHAT ARE THEY?
THEM. THOSE ARE THE THINGS I TOLD YOU ABOUT. THOSE VORACIOUS CARNIVORES FROM THAT DIMENSION I TOOK THE CHIMAERA TO. LIKE WALKING PIRANHA. THEY'VE...THEY'VE GOTTEN INTO BEDLAM.
UM, I DON'T MEAN TO INTERRUPT, YOU GUYS, BUT, LIKE, ARISA'S STILL DYING BACK HERE?!
HER RESPIRATION IS, LIKE, REALLY LOW! THE ASWANG TORE HER UP AND SHE NEEDS BLOOD...
...FAST!
I HAVE BLOOD! I HAVE LOTS OF BLOOD. 'RISA CAN HAVE IT ALL!
I DON'T MIND.
THAT'S GOAT'S BLOOD, CHOOPIE.
SO?
SHE NEEDS REAL BLOOD, CHOOP.
WELL, BIG, YOU'RE A BIG GUY. YOU MUST HAVE, LIKE, GALLONS YOU COULD LEND HER...RIGHT?
CHOOP, SHE NEEDS HUMAN BLOOD. YOURS AND MINE WON'T DO.
WE NEED TO GET HER BACK TO-
BUT, WAIT! WHAT ABOUT...
OH.
UH...

AND...UH... IT NEEDS TO BE THE SAME TYPE.
WE NEED TO GET HER TO THE MEDLAB TO LOCATE A MATCH.
OR PERHAPS NOT.
IT APPEARS THOSE CREATURES ARE EVERYWHERE. THEY'VE INSINUATED THEMSELVES INTO NEARLY EVERY LEVEL OF BEDLAM.
EVERY...?
BUT, BIG-- JOANN'S DOWN THERE! AND THE CHIEF! AND KEITH!
AND IF THEY'VE GOTTEN INTO THE MEDLAB, HOW CAN WE GET ARISA-
DEEP BREATH, MOLLY. IT'S GOING TO BE FINE.
ARISA IS PRIORITY ONE. SHE NEEDS MEDICAL ATTENTION AND WE CAN'T GET IT AT HOME. SHE'LL NEED TO GO TO A HOSPITAL.
OBVIOUSLY, THE THREE OF US CAN'T ESCORT HER THERE, SO THAT RESPONSIBILITY HAS TO FALL TO MG.
LISTEN, MG...
IN THE SHORT TIME WE'VE WORKED TOGETHER I'VE DONE MY BEST TO RESPECT YOUR PRIVACY AND YOUR DESIRE TO KEEP YOUR PAST TO YOURSELF.
BUT I DON'T LIVE IN A VACUUM AND THERE'VE BEEN TIMES WHEN I'VE OBSERVED WHAT WOULD INDICATE SOME...EXTENSIVE MEDICAL TRAINING...?
I'M SORRY. IF IT WEREN'T ARISA'S LIFE WE'RE TALKING ABOUT, I WOULDN'T ASK, BUT...
N-NO. ... YOU'RE RIGHT...
YOU'RE RIGHT.

GOOD. GREAT. MOLLY, CHOOPIE, AND I WILL DEPLOY AND ACCESS ONE OF THE REMOTE ENTRANCES TO BEDLAM.
WE'LL SEE WHAT WE CAN DO TO HELP ONCE WE GET THERE.
MG, THE NEAREST HOSPITAL WITH A SPECIALIZED TRAUMA CENTER IS HERE... BECKERTON. YOU SHOULD BE ABLE TO FIND HELP THERE.
MOMENTS LATER--
BYE, 'RIS. GET BETTER.
HERE, TAKE IT. YOU MIGHT NEED IT.
THANKS, CHOOP.
OKAY, ARISA-- STAY WITH ME. WE CAN DO THIS. WE CAN DO THIS!
HA!
AND I'M S'POSED TO DO THIS WITHOUT CAUSING PANIC OR SUSPICION...?! RIGHT.
AS I DRIVE MY UFO UP TO THE EMERGENCY ROOM DOOR AND-
OH.
HELIPAD.
OKAY.

"I CAN DO THAT."
VUMMMMMM
ELSEWHERE--
WE PLACED SEVERAL OF THESE DIMENSIONAL "BACK DOORS" INTO THE SYSTEM FOR SITUATIONS EXACTLY LIKE THIS.
THIS SHOULD OPEN UP INTO MAINTENANCE SUB-LEVEL 5.
LET'S HOPE THAT THOSE THINGS HAVEN'T MADE IT DOWN THAT FAR...
TIK TIK TIK
CLEAR.
THIS WILL SHOW WHERE THOSE CREATURES HAVE PENETRATED AND WHERE IT'S STILL SAFE.
YIKES. THEY'RE REALLY MOVING.
OKAY, HERE'S WHAT WE'LL DO...

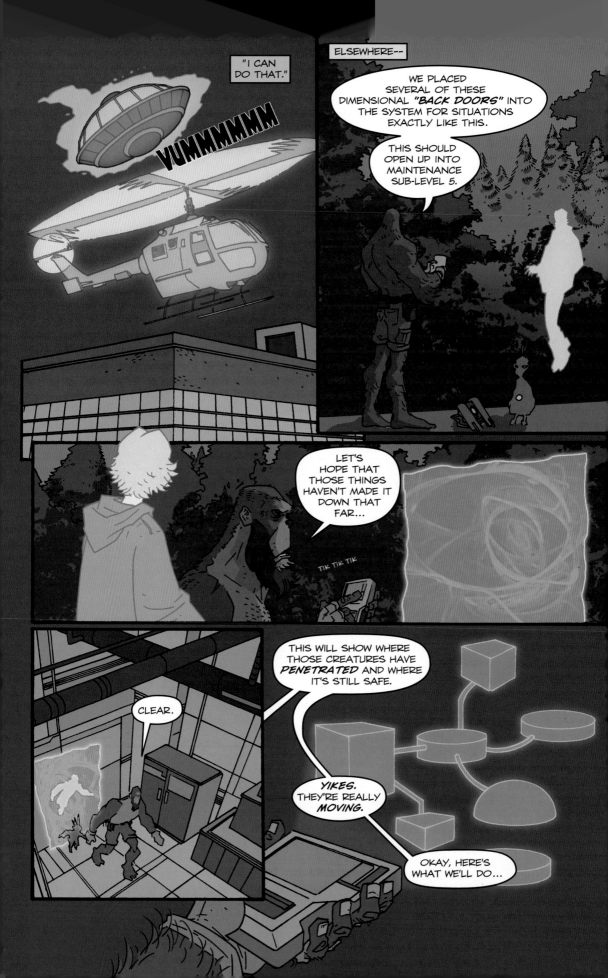

CHOOPIE--*YOU* ARE A *SECRET AGENT*. JOANN IS IN THE CHIEF'S OFFICE. I NEED *YOU* TO GO THERE, THROUGH THE DUCTWORK, CHECKING ALONG THE WAY FOR A *CLEAR ROUTE*. I WANT YOU TO BRING HER TO COMSEC...*ONLY* IF IT IS *100% CLEAR!*

WHAT WAS THE MOST IMPORTANT PART OF THAT SENTENCE?

GOOD. MOLLY-- EVERY CULTURE HAS IT'S *GHOST* STORIES. MOST ARE *FEARFUL* OF THEM. WE DON'T KNOW, BUT WE'LL ASSUME THAT *THESE* THINGS ARE, TOO. THEY CAME THROUGH THE D-GATE IN THEATER B. I NEED YOU TO SNEAK UP BEHIND THEM IN *TOTAL INVISIBILITY* AND SEE IF YOU CAN *SCARE* THEM BACK THAT WAY.

I KNOW YOU CAN DO IT.

I'M GOING TO MAKE MY WAY TO COMSEC TO SEE IF I CAN GET A BETTER PERSPECTIVE ON *WHERE* THESE THINGS ARE...AND *WHAT* WE NEED TO DO TO SEND THEM HOME.

S-SCARE...?

100% CLEAR. ROGER.

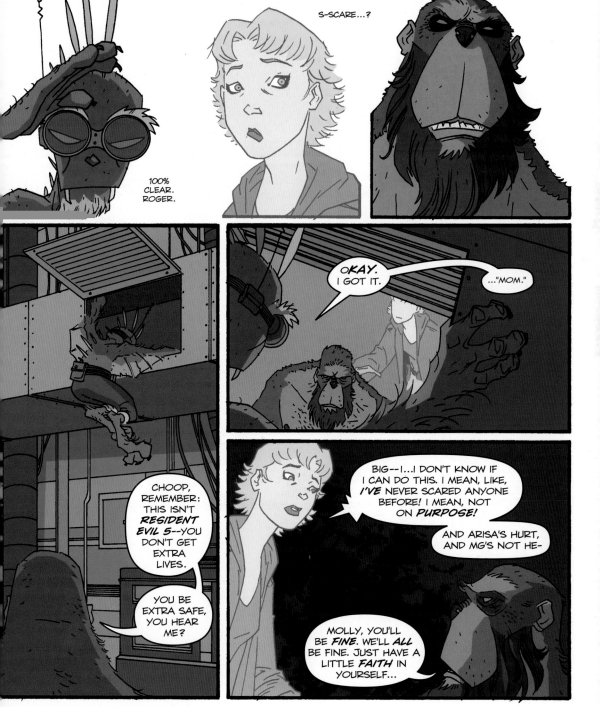

OKAY. I GOT IT.

..."MOM."

CHOOP, REMEMBER: THIS ISN'T *RESIDENT EVIL 5*--YOU DON'T GET *EXTRA LIVES.*

YOU BE EXTRA SAFE, YOU HEAR ME?

BIG--I...I DON'T KNOW IF I CAN DO THIS. I MEAN, LIKE, *I'VE* NEVER SCARED ANYONE BEFORE! I MEAN, NOT ON *PURPOSE!*

AND ARISA'S HURT, AND MG'S NOT HE-

MOLLY, YOU'LL BE *FINE.* WE'LL *ALL* BE FINE. JUST HAVE A LITTLE *FAITH* IN YOURSELF...

"...I DO."
I CAN'T DO THIS. I CAN'T DO THIS. I'M GONNA SCREW IT UP. FOR ARISA. FOR JOANN. BIG IS GONNA BE DISAPPOINTED...
SCARE THEM?! I MEAN, LIKE, HOW'M I S'POSED TO SCARE THEM?
THEY SCARE ME!
EVEN THOUGH THEY SHOULDN'T.
'CAUSE, LIKE, I'M IMMATERIAL, RIGHT? THEY CAN'T EVEN TOUCH M-
HUH?!
CLICK-CLICK -CLICK CLICK-CLICK CLICK
THAT LIGHT...? WHAT'S GOING ON IN-
CLICK CLICK-CLICK-CLICK
IT'S THEM!
WELL, SOME OF THEM...
BUT...
...WHAT ARE THEY DOING?

THEY'RE...I THINK THEY'RE TRYING TO CHEW THROUGH THE DOOR!
...HOPEFULLY WON'T RUN INTO A HORDE OF THOSE THINGS BEFORE I CAN GET TO-
COMSEC
SHUUUSHHH
eldritch
cryo
tash
WHA...?
THAT'S...
BUT THE PLACE WAS OVERRUN WITH THEM. NOW THE HALLS ARE EMPTY, MONITORS SHOW NOTHING.
WHERE COULD THEY ALL HAVE GONE?
I CHANCE TO SAY THAT THAT WILL BE THE LEAST OF YOUR SURPRISES TODAY.
EH?

WHO-?
BUT... I...
YOU'RE...
...ME!
HELLO, NAKANI.
I HAVE TO TELL YOU THAT I'VE BEEN LOOKING FORWARD TO BEING ON THIS SIDE OF THIS ENCOUNTER FOR A LONG TIME.
I KNOW FROM EXPERIENCE THAT THIS IS SOMETHING OF A SHOCK, SO I'LL GIVE YOU A MOMENT TO TAKE IT ALL IN.
UH...
...THANK YOU.

EXIT
HELLO?!
I NEED SOME HELP HERE!
I'M A DOCTOR. I WAS TRANSPORTING MY PATIENT TO BE--UH... BETHLEHEM HOSPITAL WHEN SHE STARTED TO CRASH.
I'LL NEED TO USE YOUR FACILITIES TO STABILIZE HER AND THEN WE'LL BE OUTTA YOUR HAIR.
UH...
WHOA! HOLD ON THERE, SHADES-- WE DON'T WORK THAT WAY.
SINCE WE DON'T KNOW YOU AND WE'RE NOT AFFILIATED WITH THE HOSPITAL YOU MENTIONED, I'M AFRAID WE'RE GONNA HAVE TO TAKE IT FROM HERE.
HOSPITAL RULES.
MMM. PERHAPS MY I.D. WILL OPEN SOME DOORS HERE...?
THAT'S JUST A BLAN-
OH! WOW. JOHNS HOPKINS AND THE MAYO...
STILL AND ALL, DOCTOR, UMM... RAMORAY-- WE CAN'T JUST-
WHY ARE WE STILL DISCUSSING THIS?! THIS GIRL NEEDS TO BE TYPED!
SHE HAS A DEEP LACERATION ON HER RIGHT SHOULDER! WE NEED TO START FLUIDS--

GIVE ME 2 LARGE BORE IV, A SUTURE KIT AND...
...AND WHY ISN'T ANYBODY DOING SOMETHING ABOUT THAT LIGHT?!
CLICK
BEAM
SWEEP
WHAT LIGHT...?
WHAT'S WRONG WITH THE-
LIGHT?
FUMPP!
ONE MINUTE. HATE TO WASTE EVEN THAT, BUT HOPEFULLY, WHEN THEY COME TO, THEY'LL EACH THINK THAT THEY HAD A MINI BLACKOUT AND GET RIGHT TO WORK HELPING ME.
NOW IF WE CAN JUST-
M...
...G...?
WHA-?
ARISA?!
MG...
WHERE...
...ARE...
...WE?

THIS IS NUTS! ACCORDING TO MG, THESE THINGS AREN'T S'POSED TO BE THAT SMART.
ARE THEY ACTUALLY ACCESSING-
NO. DOESN'T MATTER NOW. BIG SAID TO TRY TO CORRAL THEM BACK TO THE D-GATES.
EVERY SPECIES HAS SOME KINDA GHOSTS, HUH? WELL, IF THEY DIDN'T BEFORE...
...THEY'RE GONNA NOW!
RAAAAAAHHH!
!!
NEH!
NEH!
!!
WOW. I GUESS I CAN DO IT.
NEEEH!
NEEEH!
NOW TO MAKE SURE THEY KEEP HEADING TOWARD THE D-GATES AND-
A SCREAM?!

THERE DOESN'T SEEM TO BE SIGN OF THEM ANYWHERE. THEY'VE... DISAPPEARED...?
I CAN'T HEAR THEM OUTSIDE THE DOOR ANYMORE, EITHER.
NO...
...SOMETHING'S COMING.
DO...DO YOU HEAR SOMETHING?
LIKE SOMETHING... SCREAMING?
NO. IT'S... SINGING.
DUM DA DUM DUM DUM DA DUM DUM DUM DUM DUM DUM
KA-CLACK!
-DA DA!

WHAT ARE YOU DOING? YOU'RE SUPPOSED TO BE A COVERT AGENT--WHAT THE HELL WAS ALL THAT RACKET?
THAT WAS MY THEME SONG!
HI, JOANN! HI, DR. DAS. AND DR. MIKE. AND DR. TRISH.
UH, CHOOPIE, DEAR--WHAT ARE YOU DOING HERE? WHERE ARE ARISA AND THE REST OF THE TEAM?
ARISA GOT HURT BAD BY A STINKIN' VAMPIRE AND MG TOOK HER TO A HOSPITAL TO FIX HER UP. BIG IS IN SECURITY TRYIN' TO FIGURE OUT HOW TO GET RIDDA ALL THESE FREAKIN' CARNIVALS--
--AND HE SENT ME HERE TO RESCUE YOU!
HA!
HEH HEH, MMM. I'M SORRY.
HENH! HA HA HA!
BIG--HA! BIG SENT YOU-?
TO--HA! HA! HA! TO RESCUE US?!
HA! HA! HA!
YOU?!
HA! HA! HA! HA! HA! HA! HA! HA! HA! HA! HA! HA! HA!
I KNOW THAT KINDA LAUGH, DR. MIKE...
...THAT'S THE KINDA LAUGH WHERE A LITTLE PEE COMES OUT.

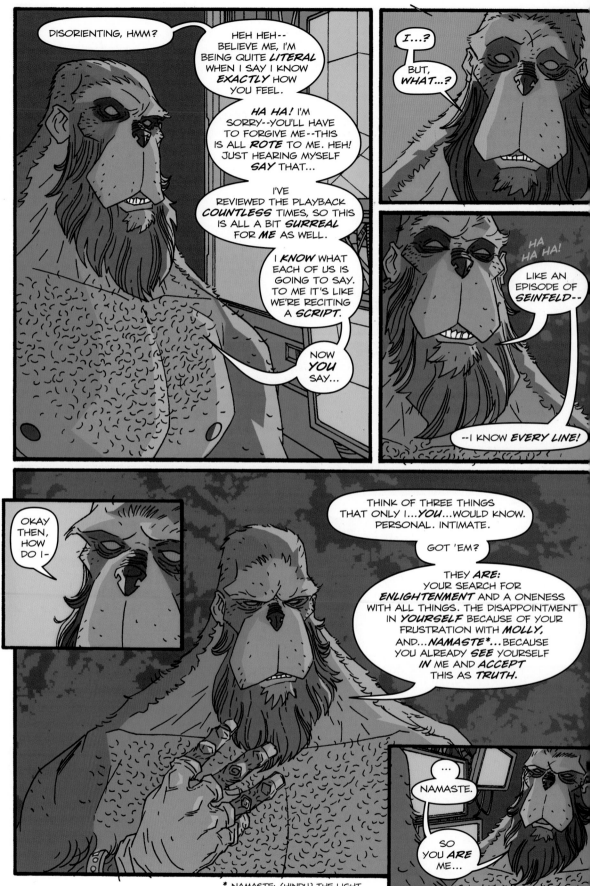

* NAMASTE: (HINDU) THE LIGHT IN ME HONORS THE LIGHT IN YOU.

--WE'VE MANAGED TIME-TRAVEL THEN?
YOU HAVE! YOU WILL. AND I KNOW YOU HAVE CONCERNS AS TO THE PRUDENCE OF THIS MISSION.
TIME IS A FRAGILE BIT OF MACHINERY. NOW THAT WE HAVE THE ABILITY TO MOVE THROUGH IT, WE MUST RESPECT THAT EVERYTHING HAPPENS FOR A REASON. EVERYTHING...
TAK TAKKA TAK
"...EXCEPT THIS!
"THE SKORM'S INFILTRATION OF BEDLAM IS AN ANOMOLY--AN UNNATURAL HICCUP IN THE CHRONAL PLUMBING."
THEY'RE NOT SUPPOSED TO BE THERE. EVER. IN ANY TIMELINE. IN ANY REALITY.
SOMEONE OR SOMETHING LET THEM IN. TO DESTROY US.
ORIGINALLY, THERE WERE FEW SURVIVORS. IN 47 OUT OF 50 CG SIMULATIONS, THEY COMPLETELY DEVOURED US, MOVING OUT INTO THE WORLD AND FINALLY REQUIRING MILITARY FORCE TO STOP THEM.
"WE MADE THE DECISION--NOT ONLY TO COME BACK AND STOP THEM, BUT ALSO TO REMIND YOU TO DO SO IN THE FUTURE."
I'M FROM THE NEAR FUTURE, NAKANI. I WON'T TELL YOU WHEN. YOU'LL KNOW WHEN.
I WILL TELL YOU THAT I...YOU...WE ARE SOON TO HAVE A REVELATION. SORRY, IT'S NOT THE SPIRITUAL ONE YOU'RE HOPING FOR. IT'S MORE ON THE SCIENTIFIC SIDE OF THINGS. BUT IT'S STILL ONE THAT COULD HAVE RAMIFICATIONS ON THE ENLIGHTENMENT OF ALL HUMANITY.
I ENVY YOU THIS EPIPHANY, BIG. IT IS A MILESTONE IN OUR LIFE. AND IT IS SO CLOSE. AND SO WONDERFUL.

IS THAT...
KARL...?
YES...
"...IRONICALLY."
GOOD JOB, KARL-- YOU'RE DOING GREAT! KEEP THE PRESSURE ON 'EM--JUST LIKE BIG SAID! KEEP DRIVING 'EM BACK!
RIGHT, PETER...?
HUH? OH, YEAH. GREAT JOB, KARL! KEEP IT UP!
UMMM...
...THANKS!
YEAH, HE'S NEVER GONNA GET USED TO YOU BEING NICE TO HIM.
HOW ABOUT YOU?
I'M ADJUSTING.
QUIET, NOW. HERE COMES YOUR GIRLFRIEND. AND WE DON'T WANNA MAKE HER JEALOUS.
This is the last one, Arisa--
?
--We can now herd the Skorm down through the DI corridor!

GREAT, MERROW!
OKAY, EVERYBODY! PUSH AHEAD! MERROW'S GOT THE CORRIDOR CLEAR!
CHOOPIE, REMEMBER WHAT BIG SAID--NO DISTRACTIONS! FOCUS!
AND HAMMERSKOLD-- WELL, YOU KNOW WHAT YOU HAVE TO LOOK OUT FOR...
WHAT WAS THAT SCREAM? I-
A...ARISA...?
HOW...
HUH?
M-MOLLY?
RIS! HOW DID YOU-
YOU'RE OKAY?
OH, GOD...
MOLLY.
ARISA! COME ON! STAY WITH THIS!
HUH?
ARISA!

ARISA?!
HEE HEE! DON' SAY IT OUT LOUD, MG...THING IT! INYER HEAD.
THESE PEOPLE-
THESE PEOPLE ARE STUNNED. I'M HOPING THAT THEY'LL EACH THINK THAT THEY BLACKED OUT FOR A SECOND AND START HELPING ME FIX YOU! BUT YOU HAVE TO-
WAIT! I C'N DO THAT, MG! I C'N BUMP 'EM ALL SO THAT THEY THING JUS' THAT! HANG ON A SEC-INT.
ARISA! WAIT!
SEE? DONE. I DID IT. HEE HEE. I TOL' 'EM THAT THEY JUS' BLACKED OU' FER A SEC, AND THAT YOU WERE A VERY FAMOUSLY IMPORTANT DOCTOR, AN' THAT THEY NEED T'HELP YOU ABOVE ALL. I ALSO TOL' 'EM THAT THESE ARE NOT THE DROIDS THEY'RE LOOKING FOR. HEE HEE. GEDDIT?
YES, OBI-WAN. YOU'RE HILARIOUS.
BUT LISTEN, ARISA, YOU NEED TO RELAX, YOU NEED TO REST.
YOU'VE GONE THROUGH SOME SERIOUS TRAUMA. YOUR BODY'S IN SHOCK AND YOU'RE UNCONSCIOUS!

I'M CONSCIOUS!
THIS'S MY SUBCONSCIOUS!
THIS'S IS THE TRUTH!
THIS IS THE PURE ME!
ARISA, YOU NEED TO REST--EVEN SUBCONSCIOUSLY. YOU SMACKED YOUR HEAD AND YOU'VE LOST A LOT OF BLOOD! YOU'RE DELIRIOUS AND YOU DON'T-
EM-GEE, EM-GEE, EM-GEE-- I'M GONNA BE FINE.
YOU WORRY TOO MUSH! WHY DO YOU DO THAT? WHY DO YOU WORRY?
I MEAN, LOOKIT THIS. LOOKIT THIS! THIS IS RIDICULOUS!
THESE DOORS ARE SO THICK! AN' YOU'VE GOT 'EM LOCKED UP SO TIGHT!
WHAT COULD YOU POS'BLY HAVE BURIED AWAY IN YOUR PAST THA'S SO HORRIBLE?!
C'MON, MG-- ERRRNT!
WHAT ARE YOU HIDING IN THERE?
HEE HEE...
CLANG! CLANG!
I DIDN'T...
I DON'T...
ARISA! THIS ISN'T THE TIME FOR THIS! YOU'RE IN SERIOUS CONDITION AND-
THERE YA GO WORRYING.
RELAAAAX. I TOLDJA-- I'M GONNA BE FINE. I AM A L'IL BIT PA-SYCHIC, YA KNOW...? AN' ANYWAY, THEY'RE ALL COMIN' OUTTA THEIR STUN.
LOOK!

CALL IT, DOCTOR. WE'RE AT YOUR DISPOSAL.
OH! UH... I NEED...SHE NEEDS IV ACCESS FOR NORMAL SALINE--2 LITERS, WIDE OPEN!
SOMEBODY CAN START ON THAT LAC ON HER RIGHT SHOULDER--MULTIPLE LAYER CLOSURE.
YOU'LL NEED SOME POLY-ZORB, 4.O.
SEE, MG? I TOLDJA. FINE!
LOOKS LIKE WE'RE GONNA NEED 4 UNITS OF TYPE A...
EVE'YBODY'S TAGIN' CARE A' ME--
YOU'RE TAGIN' CARE A' ME!--
YOU WON' LET ANYTHING HAPPEN TO ME...
...RIGHT?
YES, HELLO?
YES. I BELIEVE I HAVE SOMEONE HERE YOU'RE LOOKING FOR...

SO THE MYS'ERIES JUST KEEP COMIN'...
A DOCTOR, HUH...?
I DON' SEE WHY THAT HADDA BE A BIG SECRET...?
BUT YOU LET THAT SECRET OUT FOR ME, DIN'TCHOO?
T'TAKE CARE A' ME...
SEE? NOW WUZZAT SO HARD...?
B.P.'S DROPPING, DOCTOR.
42
I KNOW YA LIGE ME, MG.
I DON' NEE' T'BE A MINE READER T'SEE THAT!
SHE'S CRASHING!
DOCTOR? WHAT'RE YOU GOING TO DO?
DR. RAMORAY?!
BUT YA GOTTA LET ME IN, MG-- YA GOTTA TRUS' ME...
I TRUS' YOU! I TRUS' THAT YER GONNA PROTEC' ME, AN' TAKE CARE A' ME, AN' YER NOT GONNA LET ME-
WE'RE LOSING HER! WE'RE LOSING HER!
WE'RE NOT LOSING HER! WE CAN'T LOSE HER! I'M TALKING TO HER! SHE'S RIGHT-
?
to be continued

SECOND CHANCES
CHAPTER TWO

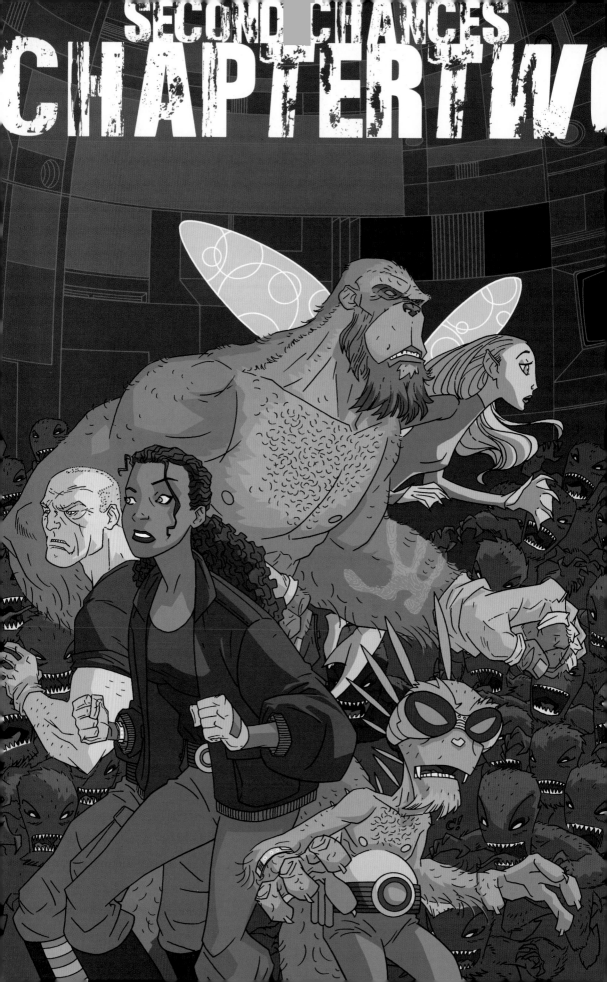

...AND WHAT HAPPENED THEN?
WELL...UH, THEN HER, UH, BP DROPPED AND SHE STARTED TO CRASH. DR...UM, RAMORAY, WAS IT? HE SAID "SHE'S NOT CRASHING." BUT THEN HE KINDA...
...FROZE UP. HE HAD A...BLANK LOOK ON HIS FACE, ALTHOUGH WHO COULD TELL BEHIND THOSE SUNGLASSES. ANYHOO, HE WAS IN THIS...TRANCE FOR ALMOST A MINUTE AND I WAS GETTING READY TO STEP IN WHEN...
...THERE WAS THIS BURST OF PURPLE LIGHT AND-
AND IS THAT WHEN YOU REALIZED THAT SHE WAS A ROBOT?
W-WHAT...? A ROB--NO. NO. YOU...YOU PEOPLE ARE CONFUSING ME. I ALREADY TOLD YOU...
THERE WERE NO ROBOTS, NO EVIL DOPPELGANGERS, AND THE GIRL DIDN'T HAVE SIX ARMS! WHY DO YOU KEEP INSISTING THAT-
THAT'S FINE, MA'AM. WHAT HAPPENED NEXT?

THEN I WAS...
...DYING.
I WAS HER...
...AND I WAS DYING.
WE ALL WERE.
"WE WERE WITH HER. WE WERE HER. AND IT WAS SO CALM, SO PEACEFUL.
"IT WAS SO WELCOMING AND INVITING.
"AND THEN... HE WAS THERE!
ARISA! NO!
"AND THEN HE CALLED MY NAME. I MEAN, HER NAME. AND MY, HER...OUR HEART JUMPED.

"HE WAS SO...
"DEVOTED."
"HEROIC."
"REAL."
MG?
YOU CAN'T GO. YOU CAN'T! THERE'S... THERE'S STILL SO MUCH THAT YOU HAVE TO DO!
BUT... I'M SO TIRED. SO WEAK.
AND IT'S SO NICE HERE.
YOU'RE TIRED. YOU DON'T KNOW WHAT YOU'RE SAYING. YOU HAVE SO MUCH TO LIVE FOR...
LIKE WHAT?
TRUST ME.

BESIDES, IF I CAME BACK WITHOUT YOU, MOLLY WOULD HAUNT ME FOR THE REST OF MY LIFE!
NOT TO MENTION WHAT BIG AND THE CHIEF WOULD DO TO ME.
AND JOANN.
CHOOPIE, I DUNNO. IT'S STILL HARD TO FATHOM WHAT THAT LITTLE FREAK WILL-
WHAT ABOUT YOU, MG?
WOULD YOU MISS ME?
YES. I WOULD.
VERY MUCH.
?
SHE'S... SHE'S COMING AROUND.
GOOD, UMM... GOOD JOB, EVERYBODY.
SEE? I TOLDJA I WAS GONNA BE FINE...

WAIT! DOCTOR, YOU CAN'T TAKE-
THANK YOU ALL. THANK YOU VERY MUCH.
"BUT THEN SHE WAVED HER HAND AND WE COULDN'T MOVE. IT WAS LIKE SHE... HYPNOTIZED US."
LIKE THIS...?
UNH.
I'M-I'M SORRY... WHO WERE YOU GENTLEMEN AGAIN...?
NO ONE, MA'AM. JUST HERE TO REVIEW YOUR HEALTHCARE COVERAGE.
SURELY 'TIS MINE TURN, GREY, TO PILOT THE AUTOMOBILE?
AND THAT'S EXACTLY WHY YOU CAN'T, ROAN--
--AND WHY I DO ALL THE TALKING.
WERE THOSE... ...MEN IN BLACK?
Y'KNOW, I THINK THEY WERE.
THAT'S MESSED UP.

THIS IS CRAP, KHIAL! I MEAN, WE'RE THE C.R.I.C.K.E.T. UNIT!
CRICKETS!
AND I KNOW I DON'T HAVE TO REMIND YOU THAT THE "C.R." STANDS FOR "CRITICAL RESPONSE"!
WE WERE TRAINED FOR EXACTLY THIS KINDA SITCH; TO ENGAGE AND CONTAIN LARGE NUMBERS OF OTHERWORLDLY VARMINTS! NOT TO-
EASY, BRIAN. DON'T MAKE ME REMIND YOU WHO THE COMMANDER OF THIS UNIT IS.
WE WERE ORDERED TO STAND DOWN BY DR...BIG ...FOOT... WHATEVER WE CALL HIM...
THE ONE GUY IN THIS WHOLE CRAZY PLACE THAT ALWAYS PLAYS STRAIGHT WITH US. AND HE'S THE SMARTEST.
HE SAYS BACK OFF, THEY'VE GOT IT COVERED, I'M INCLINED TO LISTEN.
BESIDES, SOMETHIN' TELLS ME HE JUST SAVED OUR LIVES.
NOW STOP BOTHERIN' ME WITH YOUR MACHO NONSENSE AND KNOCK ON THAT DOOR.
COMMANDER FORGES. WHAT ARE YOU DOING HERE?
SIR. WE WERE ORDERED TO STAND DOWN BY DR...UH, SASQUATCH, TO COME AND SECURE THIS OFFICE, RELIEVE CHOOPIE, AND GIVE HIM-

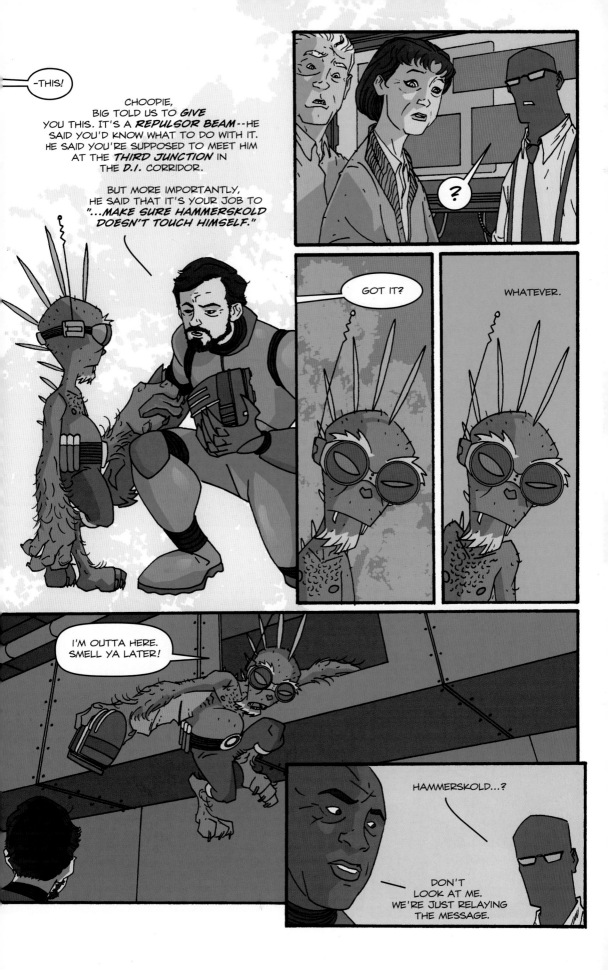

-THIS!

CHOOPIE,
BIG TOLD US TO *GIVE*
YOU THIS. IT'S A *REPULSOR BEAM*--HE
SAID YOU'D KNOW WHAT TO DO WITH IT.
HE SAID YOU'RE SUPPOSED TO MEET HIM
AT THE *THIRD JUNCTION* IN
THE *D.I.* CORRIDOR.

BUT MORE IMPORTANTLY,
HE SAID THAT IT'S YOUR JOB TO
*"...MAKE SURE HAMMERSKOLD
DOESN'T TOUCH HIMSELF."*

?

GOT IT?

WHATEVER.

I'M OUTTA HERE.
SMELL YA LATER!

HAMMERSKOLD...?

DON'T
LOOK AT ME.
WE'RE JUST RELAYING
THE MESSAGE.

GOOD JOB, EVERYBODY! KEEP THEM IN FRONT OF YOU! KEEP THEM IN FRONT OF YOU!
ARISA--WATCH THAT FLANK!
ARISA...?
DON'T BE TOO CONFUSED, MOLLY--
--THAT'S NOT OUR ARISA. THAT'S ARISA FROM THE FUTURE.
BIG?
TWO...?
BIGS...?
THAT'S HIS ARISA.
HI, MOLS! IT'S GOOD TO SEE YOU AGAIN, SWEETIE!
BIG... BUT...
I KNOW. IT'S A BIT CONFUSING.
AND, UNFORTUNATEL I DON'T HAVE TIME TO EXPLAIN. THE WINDOW'S CLOSING SHORTLY AND THERE'S ONE MORE THING WE NEED TO DO WHILE I'M HERE.
SORRY, MOLLY--
BUT...
--I'LL EXPLAIN MORE LATER!

...TELLIN' YOU RIGHT NOW, McCLUSKEY--YOU LET ME OUTTA THIS ROOM OR--
AND I'M TELLING YOU, COMMANDER HAMMERSKOLD. MY MEN AND I WERE ORDERED TO DETAIN YOU AND AGENT THORNTON BY DR....S-SAS...
...QUATCH.
McCLUSKEY
SAS...?
BIG?!!
HE DOESN'T HAVE THE AUTHORITY TO-
WHAT THE-?!
BLUE TEAM?! THOSE GLORY-SEEKING...! SO THEY CAN GET ALL THE CREDIT?!
I DON'T THINK SO!
THORNTON. JUST A JOLT.
GOTCHA, PETE.
AHHH!
ZZAK
UNGH!
HUH!
M'NOT GONNA LET ANY...

#@$%¢' BLUE TEAM! IF THEY THINK I'M JUST GONNA LAY DOWN AND LET THEM MONOPOLIZE ALLA THE ACTION, THEY GOT--
THAT'S IT, HINES! I'VE HAD IT WITH YOU AND YOUR--
...YOUR...
HERE WE GO.
WHA--
IT'S--
--ME!
C'MON, CHOOPIE...
NO.
SOME KINDA SHAPE-CHANGER--
--DOPPELGANGER--
--SOMETHING!

SOMETHING I'M GONNA PUT AN END TO RIGHT--
HAMMERSKOLD!
...IS A TELEPSYCHOMETRIST. HE KNOWS THE HISTORY OF THINGS WITH A TOUCH. IF HE MAKES CONTACT WITH HIMSELF, HE'LL KNOW HIS FUTURE.
HEY, YOU! HOLD IT RIGHT--
HEY! I SHOULD BE COMIN' THROUGH THAT GRATE RIGHT ABOUT--
--NOW!
KRAK!
UNGH!
NUH UH, HAMMERHEAD! HANDS OFF!
OOF!
WHOA!

YOU LITTLE $#!%!
I DUNNO WHAT YOU THINK YOU'RE DOIN', FREAK--
--BUT I'M GONNA MAKE YOU REGRET THE DAY YOU GOT IN MY WAY!
AND DON'T EVEN THINK ABOUT GOIN' FOR THAT GU--
NUMMMMMMMM
GOT 'IM!
YA OWE ME ONE, JERK.
HEY...
HMM...
WICKED!
AWESOME!

YOU'RE ME?! FROM THE FUTURE?!
OH, MAAAN...
HEY!
AM I RICH? DO I GET A SPEEDBOAT? WAIT, WAIT! NO-- I KNOW...
...HOW DO I DIE?
GOD, I AM STUPID.
WELL? COME ON, YOU CAN TELL ME.
MEANWHILE--
THAT'S IT! THAT'S THE LAST OF THEM! MERROW, GET READY TO CLOSE THE GATE!

AND SHORTLY--
...NOW THE MOST IMPORTANT THING IS FOR YOU TO REMEMBER TO DO THIS! HA HA!
'KAY. LISTEN... I CAN TELL YOU THIS 'CAUSE I JUST REMEMBERED I DO...
SSPS SPS PSSP SSPSS SPS SP SP SSPS...
SERIOUSLY, NAKANI-- GOOD THINGS ARE COMING. REMEMBER THAT YOUR REVELATION WILL BE MORE SCIENTIFIC THAN SPIRITUAL, SO KEEP YOUR MIND-- AND YOUR HEART-- OPEN TO THAT.
GET OUT!
SERIOUS? THAT'S TRUE?!
ACTUALLY, ALL OF YOU, KEEP YOUR MINDS OPEN TO EVERY POSSIBILITY!
THE CRAZIEST THINGS ARE GOING TO HAPPEN.
PEACE. AHIMSA.
WHAT...?
WAS THAT...?

SOMEWHERE ELSE...
HUMMM...
JUST REST, ARISA. TRY TO GO BACK TO SLEEP.
WHERE...?
A PLACE I KNOW. IT'S NOT IMPORTANT NOW. GET SOME REST.
BIG...?
AND MOLLY...?
ARE FINE.
EVERYTHING'S BEEN TAKEN CARE OF BACK AT BEDLAM. BIG CALLED ON THE SKIPPER'S COMMUNICATOR. I TOLD HIM WE'D BE BACK LATER TONIGHT.
BUT...
NO. NO MORE TALKING.
BUT THAT'S AFTER YOU GET SOME MORE SLEEP.

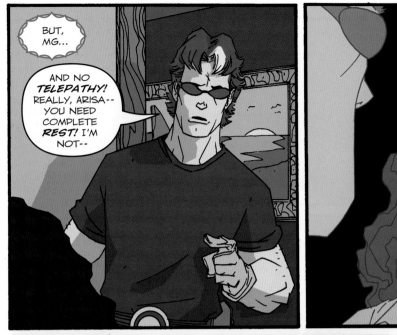

BUT, MG...

AND NO *TELEPATHY!* REALLY, ARISA-- YOU NEED COMPLETE *REST!* I'M NOT--

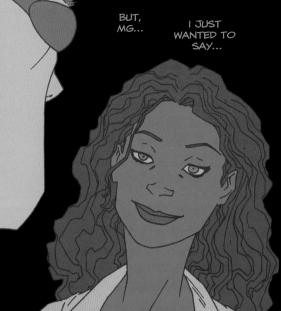

BUT, MG...

I JUST WANTED TO SAY...

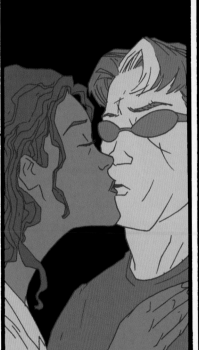

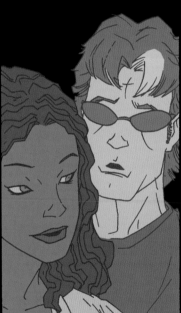

...THANK YOU.

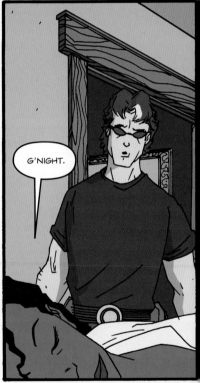

G'NIGHT.

...YOU FEEL CONFIDENT THEN, DOCTOR, THAT THERE WILL BE NO LONG-TERM RAMIFICATIONS?
WELL, SIR-- I ASSURED MYSELF THAT THERE WEREN'T ANY, SO WE ONLY REALLY HAVE MY WORD TO GO BY.
BUT YES-- ACCORDING TO THE FUTURE ME, THERE WERE NO PARADOXES CREATED...
...NO INFORMATION RELATED THAT WOULD OR COULD JEOPARDIZE THE NATURAL TIMESTREAM.
I'M SATISFIED THAT THERE WAS NO DAMAGE DONE.
WE, OF COURSE, TRUST YOUR JUDGEMENT IN THIS, BIG, AND LEAVE IT TO YOU KEEP US APPRISED OF ALL FURTHER DEVELOPMENTS.

AND I THANK YOU FOR THAT TRUST.
OBVIOUSLY, WE'LL NEED TO PLAN FOR THIS TRIP TO THE PAST IN THE FUTURE.
THOUGH WE'VE YET TO CRACK TIME TRAVEL, JUST KNOWING THAT WE'RE CLOSE...
THE BOYS IN TEMPUS ARE ALREADY WORKING ON TEMPORAL HOMING UNITS FOR TRACKING.
WE ALSO HAVE A TEAM FROM QUANTECH REVERSE-ENGINEERING THE BLAH-BLAH-BLAH...
--YOUR FRUSTRATION WITH MOLLY.
...SAPPOINTMENT IN YOURSELF BECAUSE OF YOUR FRUSTRATION WITH MOL--
WITH MOLLY.
DISA--
PPOINT--
UH.

I...
I HAVE TO GO!
MOLLY?
WHAT--
IT'S NOTHING. IT...
WHEN YOU WERE TALKING TO YOURSELF YOU SAID... YOU'RE DISAPPOINTED IN ME--FRUSTRATED WITH ME. I...I KNOW IT WAS IN PRIVATE--I DIDN'T MEAN TO--
MOLLY, THAT'S NOT--
I TRY, BIG! I REALLY DO! I WANT TO HELP, BUT... I CAN'T!
I CAN'T... TOUCH THINGS! I CAN'T...
MOLLY ... HONEY. YOU HAVE NO IDEA HOW IMPORTANT YOU ARE.
AM I?! AM I IMPORTANT?! IF I'M SO IMPORTANT, THEN, LIKE, WHERE WAS I?! WHAT HAPPENED TO ME, BIG?! HOW COME I DIDN'T COME BACK WITH THE REST OF YOU? HOW COME THERE WAS NO FUTURE ME?
WHAT HAPPENS TO ME, BIG? WHERE WAS I?
› SOB! ‹

arisa
choopie
IS AWESOME!
Choopie's room
molly

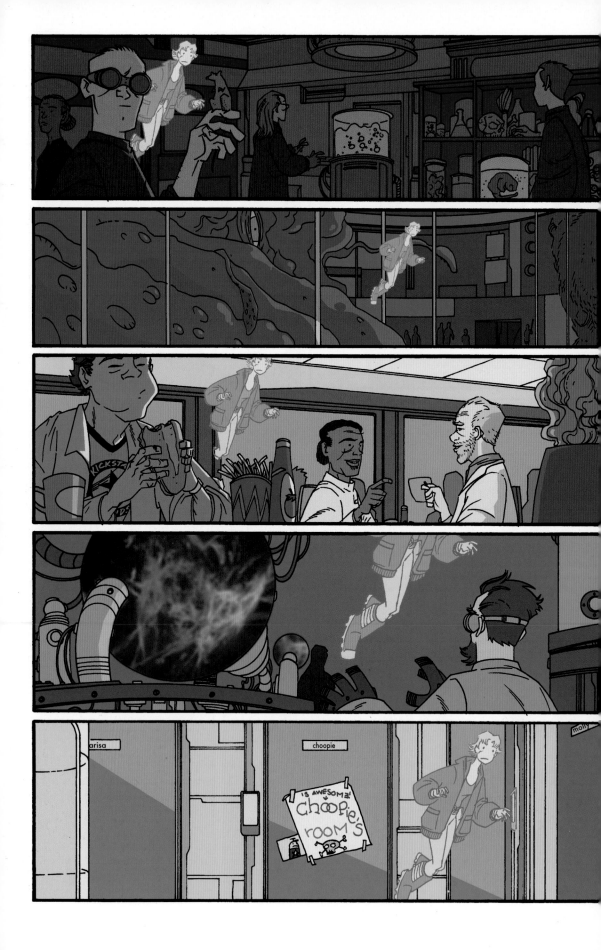

I'LL GO TALK TO HER. I WOULD IMAGINE SHE'S GONE UP TO THE APARTMENTS.
THAT'S WHERE I'LL BE SHOULD ANYONE NEED ME.
GENTLE, BIG.
TSK. CHICKS, HUH?
I KNOW YOU AREN'T PLANNING ON LEAVING THAT MESS FOR JANITORIAL! RIGHT?
OH! UH, NO. I WAS PLANNIN' ON TAKIN' CARE OF THAT RIGHT NOW.
FWINK!
CLICK CLICK CLICK
NOT THIS AGAIN.
WHAT-?!
UHNN! GIMME-- NGG! THAT--
--BACK!
OOF!
WHAT THE HELL IS THAT THING?

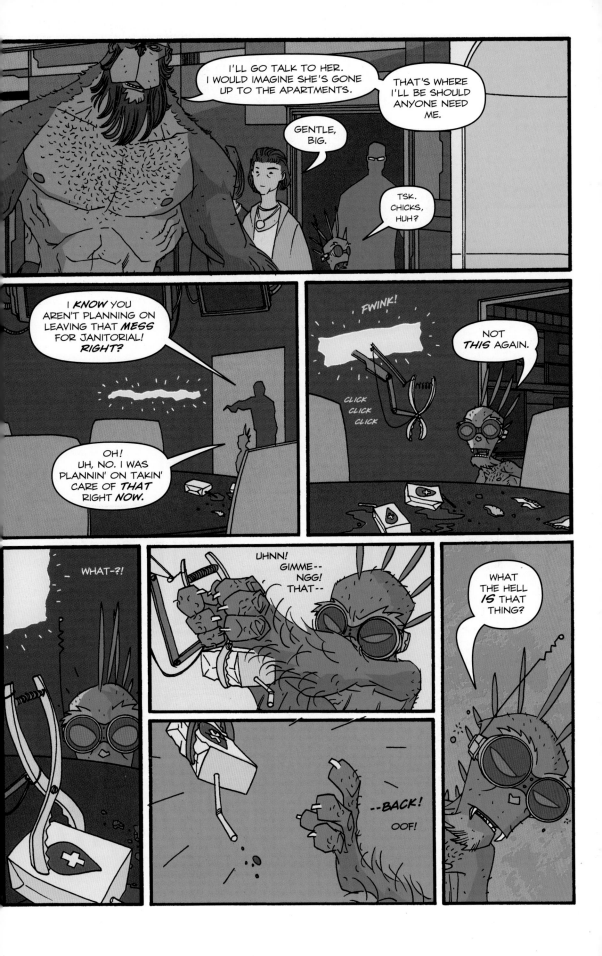

CANTELE
SELF STORAGE
sssh
UNITS AVAILABLE
Call 1-800-CAN-TELE
VWUMMMMMM!
HOLY CRAP F'CRAP!
DID WE JUST SEE THAT...?!
TO BE CONTINUED
TODD AND CRAIG'S
THE Perhapanauts
IN
HINDSIGHT
WORDS--TODD
PICTURES--CRAIG
COLORS--RICO

SECOND CHANCES
CHAPTER THREE

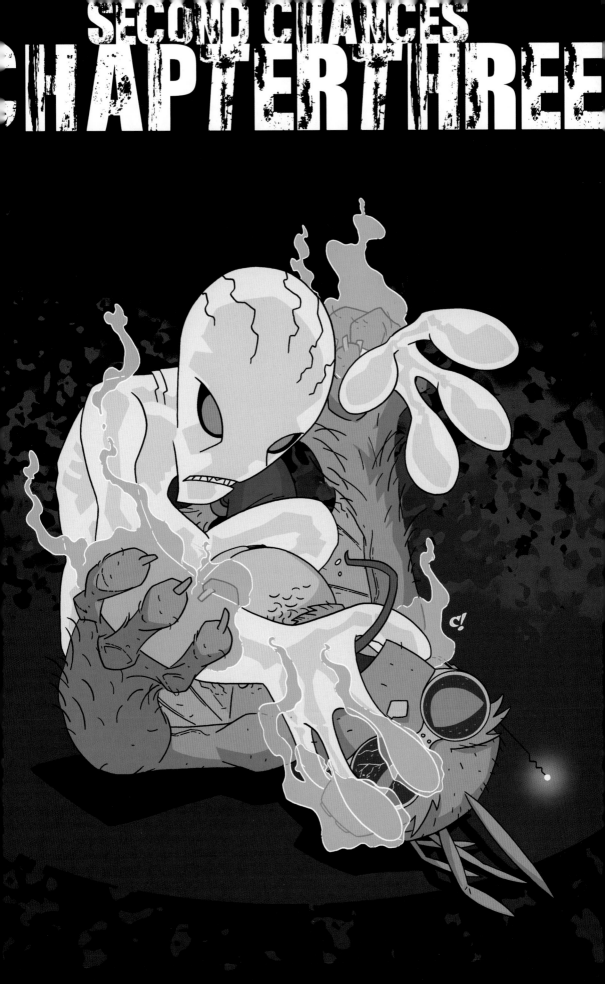

TODD AND CRAIG'S THE Perhapanauts IN

The DOVER DEMON

words by todd pictures by craig colors by rico

MOLLY...HONEY, PLEASE.
BIG, I'M SORRY. I NEVER SHOULD HAVE SAID THOSE THINGS. I NEVER MEANT THAT--I...I...
›SOB!‹
NO. NO, MOLLY. YOU WERE *RIGHT.* YOU HAVE EVERY *RIGHT* TO BE ANGRY, EVERY *RIGHT* TO BE MAD AT ME...AND EVERY RIGHT TO HAVE THE *ANSWERS* TO YOUR QUESTIONS.
MAD AT...
...*YOU?!*
BIG, I--

NO, MOLLY--PLEASE LISTEN TO ME. I WAS WRONG. I...I BECAME SO INVOLVED, SO ENVELOPED IN WHAT WAS OCCURRING, THAT I SHUT OUT EVERYTHING ELSE. I...I DO THAT SOMETIMES. MORESO LATELY.
IT... SHAMES ME.
MY SCIENTIFIC CURIOSITY BEGINS TO DOMINATE MY TRUE NATURE AND I LOSE SIGHT OF WHAT'S REALLY IMPORTANT.
THIS TIME I NEGLECTED YOU--
--MY TEAMMATE--
--MY FRIEND.
YOU MEAN TOO MUCH TO ME, MOLLY...
molly
IT HURTS ME TO KNOW THAT I'VE CAUSED YOU PAIN.
molly
I'M SORRY.
NO, I'M SORRY.

COME IN, COME IN! SIDDOWN! I DON'T HAVE MUCH TO OFFER YOU 'CAUSE, LIKE, I ONLY KEEP STUFF IN THE "REAL" FRIDGE FOR WHEN ARISA'S HERE. BUT I'VE GOT-
YOU KNOW, ASIDE FROM WHEN WE DESIGNED THIS, I DON'T THINK I'VE EVER BEEN IN HERE. IT'S NICE. DO YOU HAVE EVERYTHING YOU NEED?
EVERYTHING EXCEPT MORE COMPANY. WE SHOULD HANG OUT MORE. WE SHOULD DO MORE FRIENDS STUFF!
I KNOW YOU'RE ALWAYS DOING SOME LAB OR, LIKE, SCIENCE-Y THING...
...BUT YOU COULD COME OVER AND WATCH LOST WITH ARISA AND ME.
SIT DOWN. RELAX.
I COULDN'T SIT, MOLLY--I'D BREAK YOUR CHAIR.
NO YOU WOULDN'T. I HAD IT REINFORCED FOR WHEN YOU FINALLY DID COME OVER.
I HOPE WATER IS OKAY. I DON'T HAVE ANY SODA SINCE CHOOPIE WAS OVER OR--OH, TEA! I COULD MAKE TEA! 'CAUSE YOU'RE A BUDDHIST AND YOU GUYS LIKE TEA, RIGHT?
HA! YES, YES, I DRINK TEA. BUT WATER'S FINE, MOLLY-- MORE THAN FINE.

LET'S ANSWER SOME OF YOUR QUESTIONS, THOUGH. I DON'T KNOW WHY YOU DIDN'T COME BACK, MOLLY. YOU'RE RIGHT--I DON'T HAVE ALL THE ANSWERS. I'D LIKE TO THINK THAT YOU STAYED BACK BECAUSE MG NEEDED YOUR HELP TO OPERATE THAT TIME-GATE.
BUT I DON'T KNOW FOR CERTAIN... WE CAN'T KNOW.
I WISH I COULD GIVE YOU A BETTER ANSWER.
WHAT YOU SAID-- WHAT YOUR FUTURE SELF SAID-- ABOUT YOU BEING ...FRUSTRATED WITH ME...?
...WHAT DOES THAT MEAN?
WHAT...
NOT FRUSTRATED WITH YOU, MOLLY. FRUSTRATED WITH MYSELF.
YOU KNOW THAT I'M A SPIRITUAL PERSON, MOLLY. EVER SINCE I CAME TO BEDLAM I'VE QUESTED AFTER KNOWLEDGE. FIRST, I DEVOURED HISTORY AND THE SCIENCES, BUT I SOON FOUND THAT THAT WASN'T ENOUGH. I FELT THAT THERE WAS MORE...
I WANT TO KNOW THE MEANING OF IT ALL. WHY WE'RE HERE...AND EVERYTHING! WHAT IS OUR PURPOSE HERE ON THIS EARTH? AND I WANT TO KNOW WHERE OUR ESSENCE, WHERE OUR SPIRIT GOES...AFTER HERE.
MOLLY, I KNOW THAT YOU'RE NOT COMFORTABLE WITH YOUR...SITUATION. I KNOW YOU HAVE YOUR REASONS FOR NOT WANTING TO...GO ON, AND I TRULY RESPECT YOUR CHOICES. BUT SOMETIMES I BECOME... EXASPERATED THINKING THAT THAT KNOWLEDGE IS SO CLOSE FOR YOU.
› SOB! ‹
I'M... I'M SORRY, BIG. I--

NO, MOLLY! IT'S NOT YOU, IT'S ME! YOU HAVE NOTHING TO BE SORRY FOR! IT'S MY OVER-ENTHUSIASM! I NEED TO RELAX. I NEED TO BE AT PEACE WITH THAT.
SOMETIMES I THIRST FOR ANSWERS SO MUCH THAT I OVERLOOK WHAT'S IMPORTANT...AND WHO IT MIGHT BE AFFECTING.
I NEED TO WORK ON THAT...
HE...YOU...CALLED YOURSELF "NAKANI." IS THAT BUDDHIST?
NO. NAKANI IS ONE OF THE AMERICAN INDIAN NAMES FOR ME. FROM THE WADATOKA TRIBE. IT MEANS "WALKING BROTHER." I ALWAYS LIKED THAT AND HE...I USE IT TO REFER TO MYSELF...INSIDE, IN MY HEAD.
I LIKE IT TOO.
CAN I CALL YOU NAKANI?
I WOULD BE HONORED.
YOU CALLED ME "MOLS." MY SISTER USED TO CALL ME THAT.
DO YOU THINK... YOU KNEW THAT?
...
I DO NOW.
I JUST WANT YOU TO KNOW THAT I'M NEVER FRUSTRATED WITH YOU, MOLLY. I THINK YOU ARE A WONDERFUL PERSON AND A GREAT TEAM-MATE. AND A VERY COMPETENT AND RELIABLE AGENT.
OH, I KNOW THAT! LIKE, THAT'S WHY YOU...OR HE... SENT ME DOWN TO THE CRYPTID WING TO CORRAL THOSE SKORM-THINGS THAT WERE ACCESSING THE COMPUTER!
THE WHO-WHAT IN THE WHERE NOW?

SO, WAIT A MINUTE, MOL. YOU'RE GETTING AHEAD OF YOURSELF.
...SO THEN, LIKE, BIG AND I CHECKED THE CRYPTID COMPUTER AND FOUND THAT THE SKORM HAD CALLED UP A FILE FROM, LIKE, 1977. AND GUESS WHERE... DOVER, MASSACHUSETTS.
THEY HAD GONE SO FAR AS TO PLOT A COURSE ON THE COMPUTER, AS THE CROW FLIES, BETWEEN DOVER AND DIGHTON ROCK, A STRAIGHT LINE THAT RUNS DIRECTLY THROUGH...
...NORTON.
WHOA. YOU LOST ME. I WAS WITH YOU 'TIL "DOVER"...
YOU SAID THAT THE SKORM WERE DEVOURING THE TOP HALF OF THE CHIMAERA'S TORSO ON THE OTHER SIDE OF THAT GATE. COULD IT BE THAT IT'S ABILITY TO ADAPT COULD EXTEND THAT FAR?! THAT IT COULD-
INCREDIBLE.
I NEVER KNOW WHAT'S GOING ON.
BIG THINKS THAT, BECAUSE IT WAS SO, LIKE, ADAPTABLE, EVEN THOUGH THE SKORM ATE IT, THE CHIMAERA IS STILL WORKING THROUGH THEM, TRYING TO FINISH WHATEVER MISSION IT WAS ON WHEN WE FOUND IT AT THE FACTORY.

WE ALWAYS FELT THAT IT HAD BEEN LOOKING FOR SOMETHING...
...NOW WE HAVE AN IDEA WHAT.
I THINK WE NEED TO TAKE A RIDE.
AND I'M GOING WITH YOU. DON'T TRY TO TELL ME NO. YOU KNOW IT'S THE SMART THING TO DO. WITH HINES ON THE DL, YOU NEED MY TRAINING AND ABILITIES.
THAT'LL BE GREAT, PETER. WE'LL BE LEAVING IN AN HOUR. YOU CAN MEET US AT THE SKIPPER.
SEE YA THERE. LET'S GET READY, GANG.
UH...
RIGHT.
I, UH... I'M GLAD YOU'RE OKAY, HINES. I HOPE YOU FEEL BETTER SOON.
HEARD YOU DID A GOOD JOB OF SAVING HER LIFE OUT THERE, MG. GOOD MAN.
SEE YOU AT THE SKIPPER.
WHAT THE HELL WAS THAT?
I DUNNO.

SO...
YOU WERE
A MARINE,
HUH?

RELAX, PETER. THIS IS ONLY A RECON MISSION AFTER ALL.
I, UH...I THOUGHT THAT YOU GUYS MIGHT BE...PISSED WITH THE WAY I INVITED MYSELF ALONG LIKE THAT. I--
NONSENSE. GLAD TO HAVE YOU ALONG. I'VE ALWAYS THOUGHT WE SHOULD DO MORE OF THIS, TRADING TEAM MEMBERS. SORT OF LIKE A STUDENT EXCHANGE PROGRAM.
AND... WHAT... EXACTLY IS IT THAT WE'RE LOOKING FOR OUT HERE AGAIN, DOCTOR?
CALL ME "BIG," PETER. EVERYBODY DOES.
AND AS FOR WHAT THIS LITTLE SAFARI IS ABOUT, I'LL LET MOLLY FILL YOU IN SINCE IT WAS SHE WHO MADE THE CONNECTION IN THE FIRST PLACE.

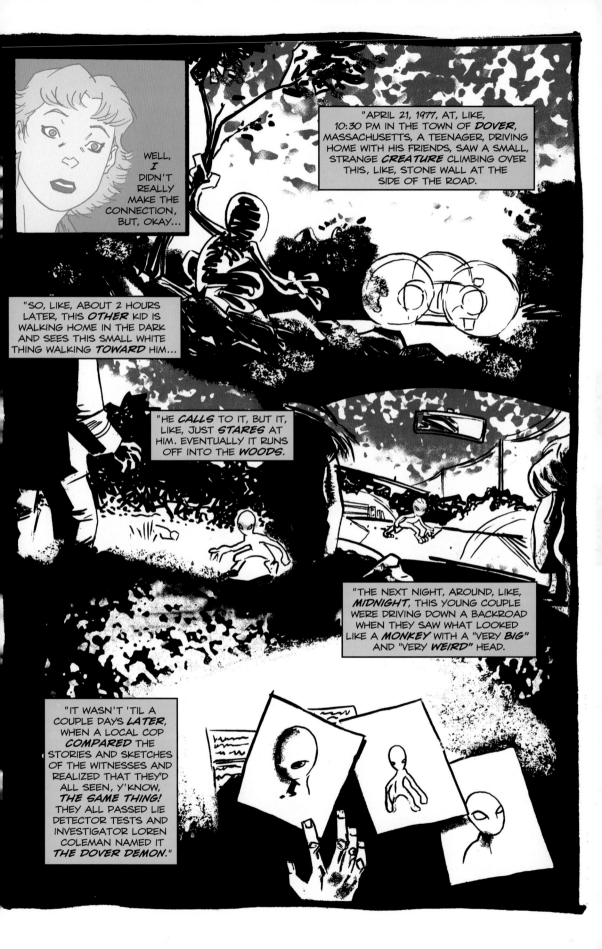

WELL, *I* DIDN'T REALLY MAKE THE CONNECTION, BUT, OKAY...

"APRIL 21, 1977, AT, LIKE, 10:30 PM IN THE TOWN OF *DOVER*, MASSACHUSETTS, A TEENAGER, DRIVING HOME WITH HIS FRIENDS, SAW A SMALL, STRANGE *CREATURE* CLIMBING OVER THIS, LIKE, STONE WALL AT THE SIDE OF THE ROAD.

"SO, LIKE, ABOUT 2 HOURS LATER, THIS *OTHER* KID IS WALKING HOME IN THE DARK AND SEES THIS SMALL WHITE THING WALKING *TOWARD* HIM...

"HE *CALLS* TO IT, BUT IT, LIKE, JUST *STARES* AT HIM. EVENTUALLY IT RUNS OFF INTO THE *WOODS*.

"THE NEXT NIGHT, AROUND, LIKE, *MIDNIGHT*, THIS YOUNG COUPLE WERE DRIVING DOWN A BACKROAD WHEN THEY SAW WHAT LOOKED LIKE A *MONKEY* WITH A "VERY *BIG*" AND "VERY *WEIRD*" HEAD.

"IT WASN'T 'TIL A COUPLE DAYS *LATER*, WHEN A LOCAL COP *COMPARED* THE STORIES AND SKETCHES OF THE WITNESSES AND REALIZED THAT THEY'D ALL SEEN, Y'KNOW, *THE SAME THING!* THEY ALL PASSED LIE DETECTOR TESTS AND INVESTIGATOR LOREN COLEMAN NAMED IT *THE DOVER DEMON.*"

SO THAT'S WHAT WE'RE LOOKING FOR? THIS DEMON THING?
HARDLY. IT'S BEEN 30 YEARS SINCE THE DOVER DEMON POSSIBLY PASSED THIS WAY...
...BUT THE CHIMAERA WAS LOOKING FOR SOMETHING OUT HERE AND WE'RE HOPING TO MAYBE FIND SOME NEW CLUES.
PLACE GIVES ME THE CREEPS.
ME TOO.
HEY, B... YOU'RE NOT GONNA BELIEVE THIS...
THIS BOG MUST'VE BEEN THE FACTORY'S CHEMICAL DUMP. THERE ARE DECADES WORTH OF TOXINS SATURATING THE MUD AND SILT.
I'VE CALIBRATED THIS THING TO DETECT EVEN THE FAINTEST OF RESIDUAL NON-TERRAN ENERGIES, BUT I'M GETTING MUCH MORE THAN THAT.
THERE'S SOMETHING DOWN THERE.
HMMM.

MOLLY, CERTAINLY NOT THE MOST DESIRABLE OF JOBS, BUT YOU KNOW WHAT I NEED YOU TO DO.
"MINE" THE POOL AND SURROUNDING AREA AND, LIKE, SEE IF I CAN GET A LOOK AT WHATEVER'S DOWN THERE.
PERFECT.
GREAT.
EEW.
EW.
EW.
EW.
MOLLY! WHAT ARE YOU WORRIED ABOUT?! YOU'RE INTANGIBLE. IT'S NOT AS IF YOU'RE GONNA GET ANY ON YOU.
THAT'S.
NOT.
THE POINT.
IT'S JUST THE IDEA.
EW.
AND WHAT AM I S'POSED TO SEE DOWN HERE? I CAN'T SEE A--
OH.
AWW.
LOOKIT THE CUTE LITTLE--

BIG! BIG, I FOUND IT! AND, LIKE--
--I THINK I WOKE IT UP!
sproing
spring
HEY!
DON'T WORRY! I GOT IT!

NO, CHOOPIE! NO SHOOTING! LET'S STAY CALM. THIS IS AN ALIEN LIFE-FORM. WE DON'T KNOW WHAT EFFECT YOUR STUN GUN MIGHT HAVE ON IT.
MY MESS-YOU-UP GUN...
HEY! IT'S GETTIN' AWAY!
IT'S OKAY! I'M ON IT!
CHOOPIE! WAIT! DAMN...MG, TRACK THAT THING--AND CHOOPIE--IF YOU CAN.
MOLLY, GO HIGH. SEE IF YOU CAN SEE WHERE THAT CULVERT COMES OUT.
WHADDAYA WANT ME TO DO?
STICK WITH ME UNTIL WE FIGURE OUT WHAT THIS THING IS.
IT LOOKS LIKE IT COMES OUT OVER THERE, BIG.
THERE'S, LIKE, A SUB-BASEMENT IN THE RUINS THAT MUST HAVE BEEN, LIKE, THE DRAINAGE TANKS FOR THE LAUNDRY OR SOMETHING.
I CAN'T SEE A FREAKIN' THING IN HERE!
I CAN SMELL IT, BUT I CAN'T SEE IT!

DARK ENOUGH FOR ME TO TAKE THESE STUPID THINGS OFF FINALLY!
OH, WAIT--NOW I CAN SEE IT--
--DOWN BY THE LIGHT AT THE END'A THE TUNNEL!
THAT'S IT, BIG. I CAN'T SEE ANYWHERE ELSE THAT THEY MIGHT COME OUT.
THEY WERE BOTH HEADED THIS WAY, BUT NOW THE DEMON HAS GONE OFF IN ANOTHER DIRECT-- NO--WAIT!

GREAT.
JUNCTION.
NOW WHERE THE HELL DID THAT LITTLE FREAK--
WAAUGH!
WHY YOU DIRTY BACK-JUMPIN', AMBUSHIN' LITTLE @@#%!

IF THEY'RE GOING TO COME OUT THERE, THEN LET'S POSITION OURSELVES TO--
THERE THEY ARE!
LET GO A'ME, YOU PALE-FACED, ZOMBIE-LOOKIN'--
SSSSSSSSS
OW!
OW!
OW!
OW!
AAAAHHH!
IT'S BURNIN' ME! IT'S--
GET OFFA ME!
#%$@!

OKAY, EVERYBODY. STAY SMOOTH.
CHOOPIE, ARE YOU OKAY?
YEAH... BUT THE LITTLE SMUDGE MELTED MY GOGGLES!
MY FAVORITE GOGGLES...
MOLLY-- GET DOWN THERE AND SEE THAT HE'S OKAY. MG. PETER. MOVE IN SLOWLY AND TRY TO MAINTAIN A PERIMETER AROUND IT. WE DON'T WANT--
MG, IT'S COMING UP BY YOU!
RIGHT.
GOT 'IM.
OKAY, BUDDY. IT'S GONNA BE ALRIGHT. JUST RELA-
DEE DEE DEE DEE DEE DEE DEE
WHA-!
!
WHAT--? WAIT!
NO!

BIG! WE'VE GOT CIVS!
TWO OF THEM! SMALL VEHICLE! COMING UP THE FACTORY ROAD!
PROBABLY A COUPLE OF KIDS, COMING BACK HERE TO DRINK. OR MAKE OUT. OR BOTH.
CHOOPIE--I WANT YOU TO GO AND DIVERT THEM. KEEP THEM FROM GETTING BACK THIS FAR. I DON'T WANT THEM TO SEE ANYTHING. INCLUDING YOU! STUN THEM ONLY AS YOUR LAST RESORT.
GOT ME?
AW, BIG--NO! I WANNA STAY! I OWE THAT LITTLE SQUIDGE AN' I'M GONNA KNOCK IT'S TEETH RIGHT OUTTA--
CHOOPIE!
MOLLY, HONEY, YOU GO WITH. KEEP HIM OUT OF TROUBLE.
BIG... DO YOU THINK THAT, LIKE, MAYBE...
MOLLY. PLEASE. GO.
BIG, I'M JUST SAYING THAT, LIKE, MAYBE YOU OUGHT TO--
WHAT I NEED, MOLS, IS FOR YOU TO GO AND SUPERVISE CHOOPIE.
THE THREE OF US CAN HANDLE THINGS HERE.
OKAY, LIKE, AS LONG AS YOU REMEMBER THAT THERE ARE FOUR OF YOU!

HAMMERSKOLD! IT'S COMING YOUR WAY!
ONCE I SHOW THESE SCRUBS HOW IT'S DONE, WE'LL SEE WHICH TEAM GETS--
KEEP YELLIN', EINSTEIN--YOU'RE SENDING IT RIGHT MY WAY. A GOOD HUNTER KNOWS TO KEEP STILL AND LET HIS PREY COME TO HIM.
THERE YOU ARE! NOW COME TO YOUR UNCLE PETE, YOU UGLY LITTLE--
I GOTCH--
HEY!
LOOK OUT, GENIUS! IT WENT RIGHT PAST YA!
HEY!
OH, NO. NOT THIS TIME. GOTCHA!
SORRY, FREAK. YOU'RE NOT BURNING ME. SEE, I ALWAYS WEAR GLOVES 'CAUSE--

I...
SSSSSSSSSSSSSSSSSSSSSS
OH.
I...
NO, PETER! DON'T LET--
TERRIFIED...
HE'S SCARED. HE DOESN'T KNOW WHERE HE IS OR HOW HE GOT HERE.
SO ALONE. HE WANTS TO BE HOME.
WE'RE ALIEN... MONSTERS TO HIM...
HE'S TERRIFIED.

"I BECOME SO IMMERSED IN WHAT'S GOING ON, I LOSE SIGHT OF WHAT'S *IMPORTANT*."
"AS LONG AS YOU REMEMBER THAT THERE ARE *FOUR* OF YOU!"
"...TERRIFIED..."
MOLLY SAW IT, AND WAS TRYING TO TELL ME.
THIS IS MINE. I OWN IT. AND NOW I'VE GOT TO FIX IT.
I DID THIS. I DID IT AGAIN.
I'VE ALLOWED MYSELF TO BECOME SO *FIXATED* ON SOME SCIENTIFIC *"EPIPHANY"* THAT I DIDN'T SEE THAT WE WERE *TERRORIZING* THIS LITTLE GUY.
MG--COULD YOU GO BACK TO THE SKIP AND GRAB SOME BLANKETS AND A CONTAINMENT CUBE?
IT'S OKAY, BUDDY. IT'S ALRIGHT.
NO, NO. NOT THERE. NOT--
KRAKK!
NO!
THUNT!

› NNT! ‹
› NNT! ‹
PETER?
BUT...
› NNT! ‹
...NOT FOR LONG.
› NNT! ‹
GOTCHA!
› SSST! ‹
AAAAAHH!
...HANG ON... HANG...
SLIPPING...
LOSING IT...
GOTCHA.
SSSSSSSSSSS
SOON--
IT'S OKAY, BUDDY. WE GOTCHA. WE GOTCHA.
THANK YOU.

10 DAYS LATER--
...LOWER FUNCTIONING, ACTUALLY, THAN CHOOPIE. THE ACIDIC SECRETIONS ARE NOT A CONSTANT, ONLY PRODUCED DURING TIMES OF STRESS OR FEAR. WE CAN'T BE SURE SO WE'VE KEPT HIM IN THE SUIT.
WE'VE PUT HIM THROUGH THE EVOLVO-RAY--SEVERAL TIMES ACTUALLY--WITH LITTLE OR NO RESULT. HE MAY BE AS EVOLVED AS HE'S GOING TO GET.
I'VE TRIED TO COMMUNICATE WITH HIM TELEPATHICALLY, BUT HAVE GOTTEN NOTHING--EVEN ON THE MOST RUDIMENTARY LEVELS. ONLY VAGUE EMOTIONAL SUGGESTIONS.
"SAD. LONELY. HOMESICK."
WE COULD KEEP HIM HERE, OF COURSE, MAKE HIM COMFORTABLE, TRY TO MAKE HIM HAPPY. AND I KNOW THAT THIS IS MOSTLY MY GUILT SHOWING, AND MY FRUSTRATION...
...BUT THERE'S NOTHING I'D LIKE TO DO MORE THAN TAKE THIS GUY BACK TO 1977 AND SEE IF WE CAN'T GET HIM BACK HOME.
...
HMM.
UM...
...BIG?
UH, I CAN DO THAT.
WHAT?!
NEXT ISSUE:
KARL CAN DO THAT.

THERE'S MORE...

SECOND CHANCES
CHAPTER FOU

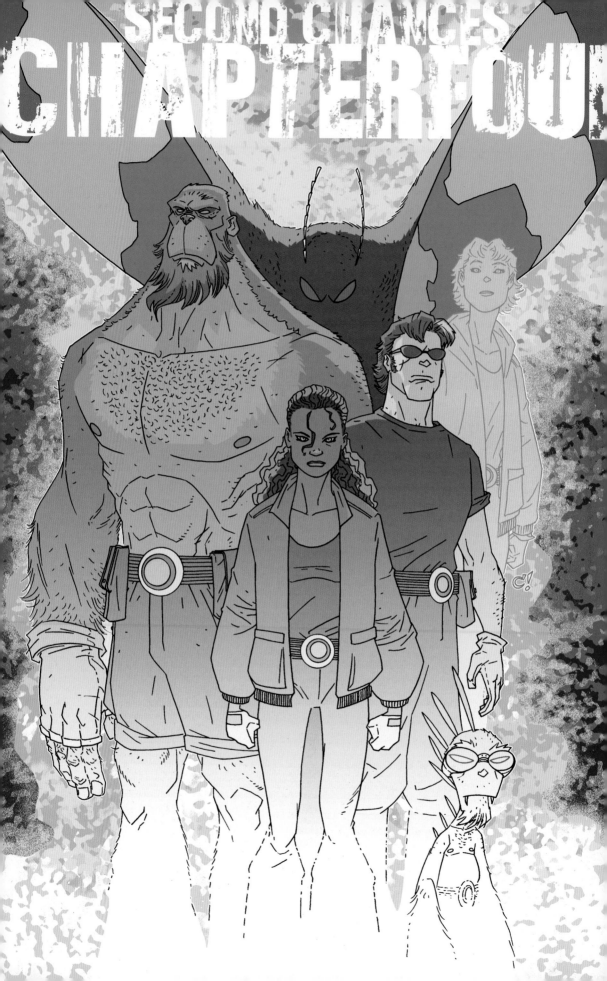

NOW--!
IT'S OKAY, DOVER. EVERYTHING'S GONNA BE FINE.
?
AT LEAST... I THINK IT IS.
OKAY, SO, IT MIGHT GET A LITTLE BUMPY NOW, BUT DON'T WORRY. WE'RE ALMOST THERE.
WE ARE AT THE DEAD CENTER OF THE BERMUDA TRIANGLE, FOLLOWING A MOTHMAN THROUGH WHAT HAS BEEN, FOR THE PAST 45 MINUTES, THE MOST INTENSE TURBULENCE EVER RECORDED BY MAN, AND HE SAYS NOW IT'S GOING TO GET A LITTLE BUMPY?
THERE IT IS, MG. YOU CAN RELEASE THE STEERING NOW; IT'LL FIND IT'S OWN WAY--
--WE JUST NEED TO FOLLOW THE WHITE LINE. OH, AND IT MIGHT BE GOOD IF EVERYBODY THINKS ABOUT ICE CREAM SUNDAES.
WHAT?! WHAT DID HE SAY?
KARL...

THEN.
I...I SAID, I CAN DO THAT.
I CAN TAKE THE LITTLE GUY BACK TO 1977 AND TRY TO GET HIM BACK TO HIS TRUE WORLD... REALM...DIMENSION... THINGY.
...WHAT DID YOU JUST SAY?!
YOU CAN? I MEAN, KARL-- YOU CAN?!
WHY DON'T I KNOW THAT? WHY DIDN'T YOU EVER TELL US?
S-SURE I CAN. AND...I THOUGHT YOU KNEW.
I DID TAKE THOSE CEMENT-EATING SLUGS BACK TO 1971 FOR YOU... REMEMBER...?
BACK IN PERHAPANAUTS: FIRST BLOOD #1--REMEMBER?
ACTUALLY, THAT BIT OF INFORMATION HAD SLIPPED MY MIND. BUT I HAD ALWAYS THOUGHT...ASSUMED, I SUPPOSE NOW, THAT YOUR TRIBE-- THAT YOU COULD ONLY TRAVERSE TIME UNACCOMPANIED. AND THOSE SLUGS WERE A MUCH SIMPLER LIFE-FORM, I-
EW!
THOSE THINGS WERE, LIKE, SO GROSS! THEY GAVE ME NIGHTMARES!
I KNOW. THOSE SLIMEY LITTLE GRUBS WERE PROBABLY THE MOST DISGUSTING THINGS I'VE EVER--
COULD WE PLEASE STOP--
--TALKING ABOUT SLUGS?!

IT'S REALLY JUST CARRYING SOMEONE ALONG WITH ME ANYWAY.
I MEAN, THE LAWS WILL HAVE TO BE ADHERED TO...
WHAT LAWS?
MY PEOPLE-- MY CLAN-- IS CHARGED WITH ABIDING BY WHAT WE CALL "THE SOO-LEES"; THE LAWS OF TIME AND THE REALITIES.
"TO ALTER NOTHING. TO CREATE NOTHING. TO HONOR THE FLOW OF THE PAR-HA."
WE ARE OBSERVERS. WE ARE GUARDIANS.
KARL, I DON'T MEAN TO QUESTION YOUR JUDGMENT, BUT ARE YOU CERTAIN THAT THIS IS THE RIGHT THING TO DO? THAT THIS IS THE TIME?
WE KNOW THAT YOU'RE ON...UNEVEN TERMS WITH YOUR PEOPLE. WE WOULDN'T WANT YOU TO DO ANYTHING THAT MIGHT... AGGRAVATE THAT SITUATION.
WE WOULDN'T WANTCHA TO, LIKE, GET IN TROUBLE.
NO, THERE WOULDN'T BE TROUBLE. THEY...THIS WOULD DISRUPT NOTHING. THAT LITTLE GUY'S BEEN IN HIBERNATION FOR THE PAST 30 YEARS. HE HAS AFFECTED NOTHING. IT WOULD CHANGE NOTHING TO RETURN HIM TO HIS TRUE WORLD MOMENTS AFTER HE LEFT.
AND LOOK AT HIM. SO SAD. HOW COULD THIS NOT BE THE RIGHT THING.

IS THAT... KARL...?
YES...
...IRONICALLY.
KARL...
...ARE YOU MY EPIPHANY...?
KARL, YOU SAY THAT YOU CAN TAKE THE DEMON BACK IN TIME. DO YOU THINK YOU COULD TAKE, SAY...
...ME?
WELL, YOU'RE KINDA BIG, BIG, BUT I GUESS I COULD. I GUESS I COULD TAKE ALL OF YOU IF THERE WERE SOME WAY TO CARRY YOU.
WHOA. WHOA. YEAH. I SEE IT.
BIG, IT'S--
WE COULD--
KARL, DO YOU SUPPOSE THAT IF I OUTFITTED YOU WITH A QUANTUM-DRIVE PAN-D LOCATOR MARRIED DIRECTLY TO THE SKIPPER'S NAV-DAP FIEPICK THAT WE WOULD BE ABLE TO FOLLOW YOU THROUGH TIME?
THAT'S EXACTLY WHAT I WAS ABOUT TO ASK.

TWO DAYS LATER--
HOLD STILL, KARL.
THANKS! OH, THANKS SO MUCH, YOU GUYS! THIS IS GREAT!
DON'T MENTION IT, KARL. WE'RE GLAD TO HELP. AFTER RICO AND I SAW THE ENERGY SIGNATURE IN THE REPLAYS OF THE "EVENT", IT DIDN'T TAKE US LONG TO FIGURE OUT WHAT WE NEEDED TO DO.
LOOK, YOU GUYS! I CAN HOLD THINGS!
I CAN REALLY HOLD THINGS!
THAT'S BRILLIANT, KARL! GREAT JOB, SCOTT, RICO.
ARE YOU READY TO GO, KARL?
AND, 45 MINUTES LATER--
KARL, THE COURSE YOU HAVE US ON TAKES US RIGHT TO THE CENTER OF THE BERMUDA TRIANGLE.
THE DEVIL'S TRIANGLE.
SHUT UP, CHOOPIE.
AND NOW--
ICE CREAM SUNDAES--OR SOMETHING!
IT'S GOOD TO RELAX AND THINK OF SOMETHING NICE.
IT MAKES THE TRANSITION EASIER.
TRANSITION?! WHAT TRANSITION?!

WHA-
AMAZING.
THIS IS THE "PAR-HA." MY TRIBE CALLS IT--
?

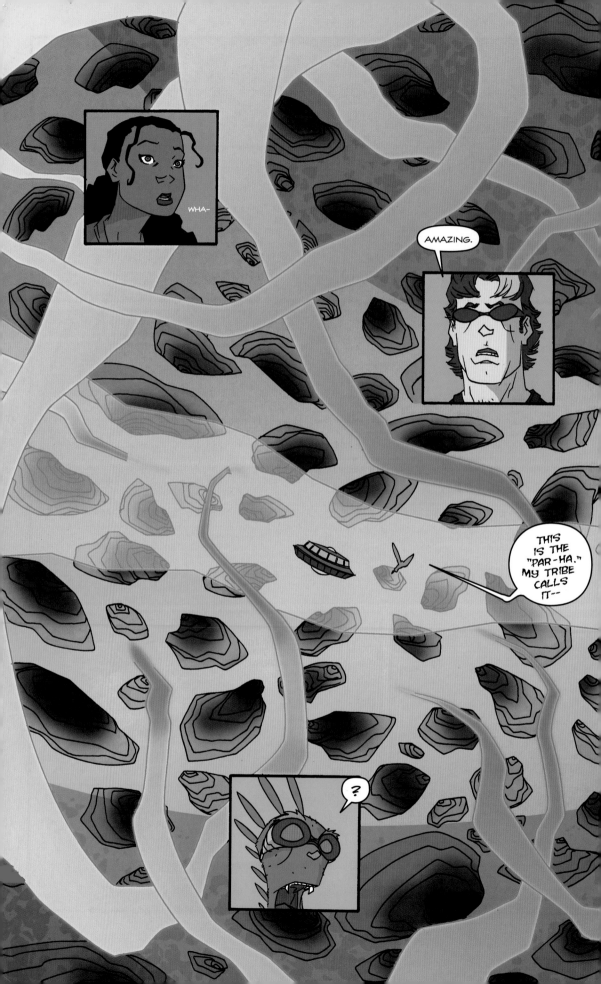

INCROYABLE.
*
IT'S SO-
THE
--THE PERHAPS!
TODD AND CRAIG'S
Perhapanauts
INTO THE PERHAPS!
words--todd pictures--craig
colors--rico

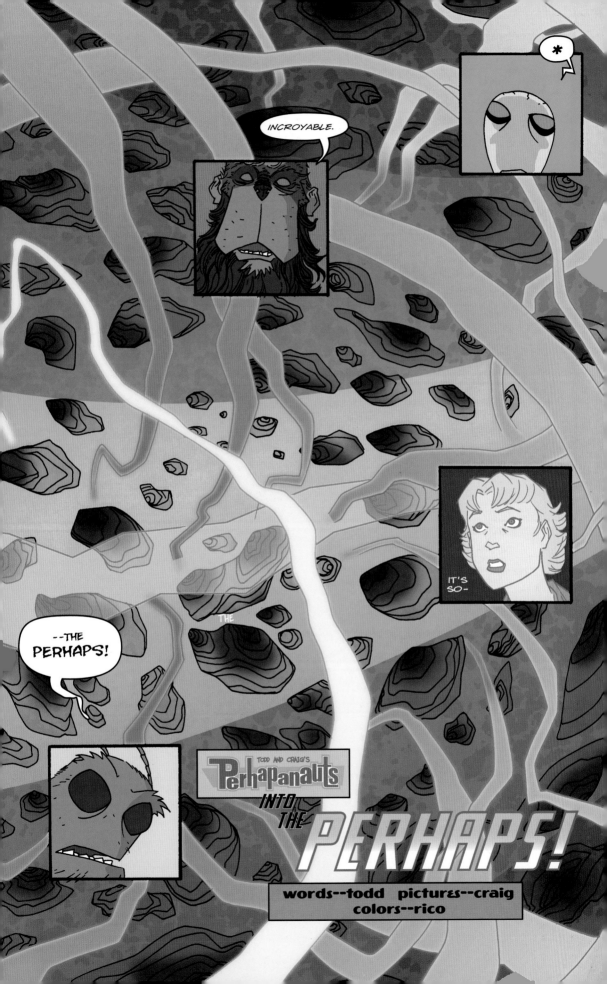

KARL...
WHAT... WHAT *IS* THIS?
WHAT'S *HAPPENING*...
...OUT THERE?
EVERYTHING.
THE PAR-HA IS THE CONDUIT THAT THE TIME STREAM TRAVELS THROUGH.
IT'S ALSO THE PLACE WHERE ALL OF THE ALTERNATE REALITIES, THE ELSE-WHERES AND THE IF-WORLDS, BRANCH OFF AND FOLLOW THEIR OWN COURSE.
IT'S EVERYTHING.

AND THAT'S DOVER'S LINE. WHAT WE'RE FOLLOWING BACK TO 1977.
C'MON! THERE IT IS! WE CAN WATCH HIM AS HE COMES THROUGH THE RIFT!
WOW! HE'S REALLY RUNNING! LIKE HE'S--
--CHASIN' AFTER SOMETHING!
M-- IS IT BIG ENOUGH? CAN YOU GET A READING ON HIS DIMENS--
ALREADY GOT IT.
KARL, CAN WE GO FARTHER BACK, TO BEFORE HE CAME THROUGH? LIKE, SAY, FIFTEEN MINUTES?
SURE, BIG.

AND, MOMENTS LATER--
OKAY, KARL... NOW!
AND HE SHOULD HAVE THE D-GATE OPEN RIGHT ABOUT...
THERE IT IS!
SO...DOVER... THIS IS YOUR WORLD, HUH? IT'S VERY... UH...
COLORFUL.
IT'S BEAUTIFUL.
IT'S SQUISHY.

AND IT SMELLS LIKE SH--
HEY! GET YER ACID-HANDS OFF ME!
YA FREAK! WHADDAYA THINK YER DOIN'?!
SNAP!
YANK!
YEAH. I THINK HE JUST SAVED YOUR LIFE, CHOOP.
HEY, YOU GUYS! LOOK AT THIS!
MORE DOVERS!
THAT MUST BE HIS FAMILY! THIS MUST BE HIS HOME!
EEE!

LOOK HOW HAPPY HE IS! HE CAN'T WAIT TO GET BACK DOWN THERE!
WELL, HE'LL HAVE TO WAIT UNTIL HE LEAVES. I WONDER WHICH--
OH, I'LL BET THAT'S HIM! THERE IN THE MIDDLE!
...PRIMITIVE, NO HAND-HELD TOOLS THAT I CAN SEE. YET THEY APPEAR TO BE HARVESTING AS A COLLECTIVE. DO YOU SUPPOSE A LOW-LEVEL HIVE MIND...?
THAT WOULD CERTAINLY ACCOUNT FOR THE LITTLE GUY'S DISORIENTATION AND INABILITY TO--
KRA-SHOOOOM!
HURRRRR!
EE!

EEE!
MY GOD! WHAT--
WE HAVE TO--
NO! YOU CANNOT! YOU CAN'T! YOU... YOU PROMISED.
YOU PROMISED.
BUT, KARL--WE CAN'T JUST STAND HERE AND WATCH WHILE THAT...CARNAGE...
YOU MUST! IT IS HISTORY!
IT'S THE LAW OF THE PAR-HA!
TO ALTER NOTHING. TO CREATE NOTHING.
WE CAN ONLY... OBSERVE.
WHAT IF YOU DO DO SOMETHING? IT'S BAD, RIGHT? 'CAUSE--
--LOOKIT MOLLY.

EVERY-THING'S AFRAID OF SOME-THING...
BACK! GET BACK!
NO! MOLLY, STOP! YOU CAN'T INTERFERE!
STOP! STOP...
BUT KARL-- IT ATE THEM ALL! AND NOW--
--NOW IT'S GOING AFTER DOVER!
MOLLY, WE CAN'T DO ANYTHING.
THIS IS WHAT HAPPENED.
BESIDES, IT'S ALMOST TIME. HE SHOULD BE GOING THROUGH THE RIFT ANY MOMENT NOW.
KARL--THERE IS NO RIFT! THERE'S NOTHING THERE! IT'S ALMOST TIME AND--
--THAT THING'S GONNA GET HIM!
NO RIFT? BUT... THERE HAS TO BE... UNLESS...

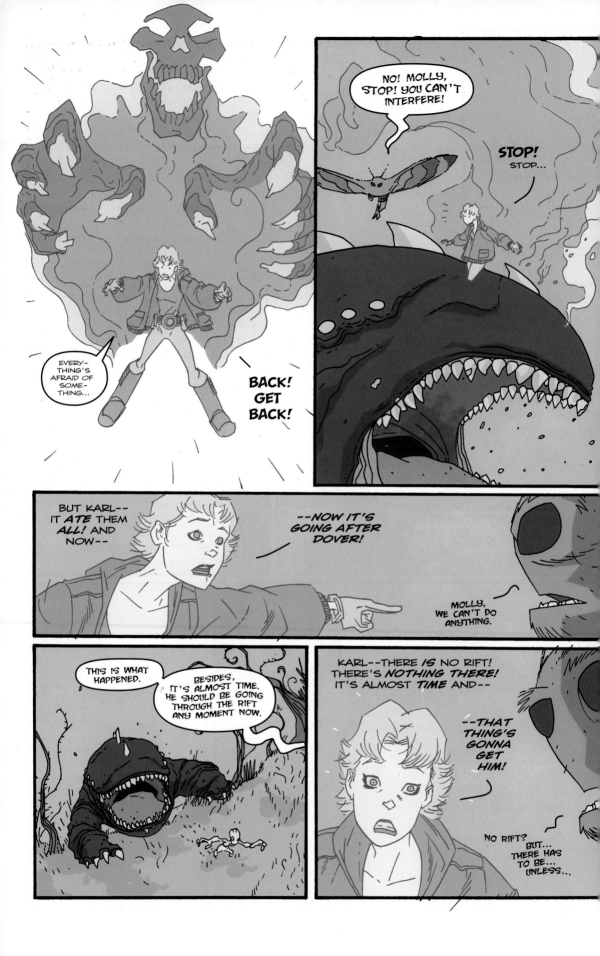

UNLESS *WE* MADE ONE.
WHAT DO YOU HAVE THERE?
SOMETHING NEW.
FFFF FFFFFFFFFFFFFFFFF
R-RAKT
CHAK
CHAK
CHAK
FFFWIMMMMMMMMM

CLOSE.
OUTSTANDING.
I'M SORRY, KARL. I KNOW WE PROMISED, BUT IT SEEMED THAT--
?
NO, MG! YOU WERE RIGHT! YOU MUST'VE BEEN! YOU MADE THE RIFT--YOU ALWAYS HAD.
I'M SORRY, LITTLE GUY. I'M SO, SO SORRY...
KARL...DO YOU THINK IT WOULD BE A PROBLEM TO TAKE HIM BACK WITH US NOW? IT WOULDN'T AFFECT THE TIME-STREAM... NOT NOW. I CAN'T READ HIS THOUGHTS, BUT I GET A "SENSE" THAT THAT'S WHAT HE WANTS.
THERE'S NOTHING LEFT FOR HIM HERE.
"THAT WOULD BE OKAY, ARISA."
THERE'S THE VORTEX, SO JUST LET THE PAR-HA PASS YOU THROUGH AND--
UM...YOU GUYS KNOW HOW TO GET BACK FROM HERE. I'VE... GOTTA GO...DO SOMETHING.
SEE YA BACK AT THE BASE.

HEY! WAITAMINNIT! DON'T I GET A SAY IN THIS...?!
THERE IS NO WAY THAT LITTLE SMUDGE IS GONNA BE ON THIS TEAM! HE DOESN'T HAVE ANY TRAINING!
I HAD TO GO THROUGH YEARS OF TRAINING BEFORE I COULD JOIN THE TEAM!
NO YOU DIDN'T.
YEAH...WELL... I'M THE GUY WHO DOES ALL THE SNEAKY STUFF!
CHOOPIE...
I GET INTO ALL THE TIGHT PLACES!
WE DON'T NEED ANOTHER LITTLE GUY!
I'M THE LITTLE GUY!
CHOOPIE, PLEASE...
AN' HE IS NOT GETTIN' A MESS-YOU-UP GUN!
AN' I AM NOT SHARING MY ROOM WITH HIM!
IF HE THINKS HE CAN JUST--
CHOOPIE! SHUT UP!
IT'S NOT LIKE THAT.

GOOD...GOOD-BYE, LITTLE GUY. AND GOOD LUCK.
WH... WHERE IS HE G...
WHAT?
than K yye ooo
HE WAS MY BEST FRIEND.

CAN
:sssh:
I'M TELLIN' YA, YOU'RE NOT GONNA FIND ANYTHING. WE'VE BEEN WATCHING THIS PLACE FOR OVER A WEEK NOW AND'VE SEEN ALL KINDSA WEIRDOS GOING IN AND OUT OF HERE. WITH THE TECH THEY'VE GOT, I GUARANTEE YOU THAT THEY'VE MADE US. AND IF THEY WERE WORRIED ABOUT US AT ALL THEY WOULD HAVE LET US--
DUDE, I CAN'T EVEN SEE A SEAM.
SSHHHHHH
...IN?
SHOULD WE BE... PREPARED?
LET'S BE FRIENDLY. IF THEY HAVEN'T MADE US, WE'LL TELL 'EM WE'RE HERE TO RENT A UNIT.
A UNIT TO STORE WHAT?
HOW ABOUT YOUR INCREDIBLY HUGE NEGATIVE ATTITUDE?
SERGENTS JAMES PETERSON AND NICHOLAS FRANKLIN--
PLEASE STEP FROM THE TRANSPORTER--
--AND KEEP YOUR HANDS WHERE WE CAN SEE THEM!
"WE'RE HERE TO RENT A STORAGE UNIT..."
WOULDA WORKED.
ASS.
YOU'RE AN ASS.
YOU'RE AN ASS.

DETECTIVES. I WON'T INSULT ANY OF US BY TRYING TO PLAY GAMES. YOU'RE OBVIOUSLY INTELLIGENT MEN OR YOU WOULDN'T HAVE GOTTEN THIS FAR. WE'VE WATCHED YOU WATCH US FOR JUST OVER A WEEK NOW, INITIALLY TRAILING A TRIO OF OUR AGENTS, WHICH, I MUST SAY, IS NO MEAN FEAT.
WE ID'D YOU SEVERAL DAYS AGO, LOOKED INTO YOUR BACKGROUNDS, AND WHILE NORMALLY WE WOULD HAVE DISPATCHED YOU ON A TRAIL OF MISINFORMATION--OR MODIFIED YOUR MEMORIES--WE ARE ALL VERY KEEN TO KNOW--
--WHAT ARE A COUPLE OF HOMICIDE/SVU DETECTIVES FROM PHILADELPHIA DOING STAKING OUT A TOP SECRET GOVERNMENT FACILITY--
--SO FAR FROM HOME?
ACTUALLY, MR...WHAT DID YOU SAY YOUR NAME WAS AGAIN...?
HEH. IN YER DREAMS.
RIGHT. WE'RE FOLLOWING UP ON A MISSING PERSONS CASE FROM A FEW YEARS BACK...
AND WE'VE RECENTLY COME TO BELIEVE, THAT YOU... UM...SPOOKY FOLKS--
--MIGHT HAVE SOME IDEA ABOUT WHERE SHE MIGHT BE.
ARISA.

SORRY.
IIII'M GONNA TAKE THAT AS A "YES."
OH, ABSOLUTELY.
sweeet sweeet sweeeet sweeet swee
INTEGRITY BREACH! INTEGRITY BREACH!
SIR, SHOULD I-
AWAIT MY ORDER, MULCAHY.
FWINK!

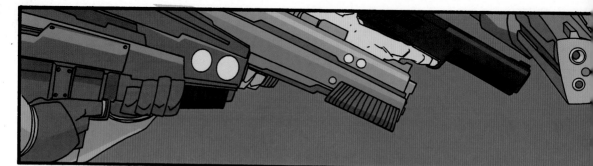

>ahem<

from the gremn, we bring to you,
the inhabits of this earthy, greetings and salmutations
from all the peoples of our placy-place. we would love
to make of all the pleasantries and cleremonies, and
especially the chat-chit, howether our mission here
is one of urgemency!
our peopulation is heavy
under the thrall of dark and lethargic
forces and we have been spatched to come
to this realm to retrieve our fortold king,
he that is destined to deliver us all and
lead us to bright futures!

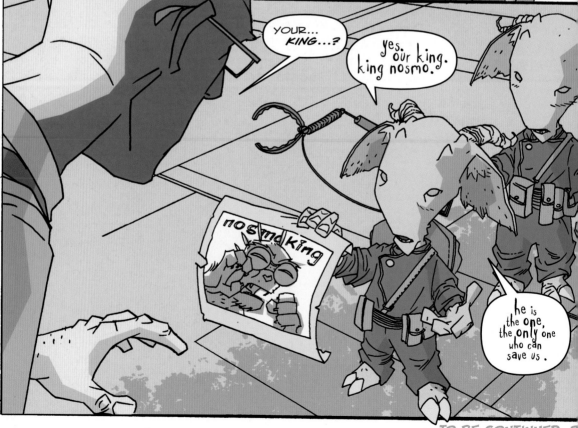

YOUR... KING...?

yes. our king. king nosmo.

he is the one, the only one who can save us.

TO BE CONTINUED...?

special bonus story!
TODD AND CRAIG'S
THE Perhapanauts
in
the first pie story!
YOU GUYS-- WE'VE BEEN DEKED! I DON'T SEE ANY SEVEN FOOT TALL MAN-MONSTER ANYWHERE AROUND HE--
...HE'S RIGHT BEHIND ME, ISN'T HE?
C!

Outside
Stockbridge, Massachusetts
4:21 am
THE STILL MORNING AIR SUDDENLY LURCHES AND SHUDDERS, SEEMING TO TWIST IN ON ITSELF... AND THEN --
FASHH
--THREE UNIQUE FIGURES APPEAR OUT OF NOWHERE!
--SS!
CHOOPIE! WATCH YOUR LANGUAGE!
WHADDA YA GOT, MOL?
WELL, LIKE, THE LOCATOR IS DEFINITELY READING AN ANOMOLY, BUT THAT'S ALL I'M GETTING...
...IT'S NOT TELLING US WHAT IT IS... OR WHERE!
I'M JUST READY TO KICK ME SOME BAD ANOM'LY BUTT!
HOW DO THEY EXPECT US TO FIND THIS THING IF, YA KNOW, WE DON'T--

EEEEEEEEEEEEEEE!
OH, WELL... YEAH...
...I GUESS WE COULD ALWAYS JUST, LIKE, FOLLOW THE SCREAMS.
I WISH 'RISA WAS HERE-- I HATE BEING FIELD LEADER.
YOU'LL BE FINE, MOL. STOP WORRYING.
O-OKAY... I GUESS... LET'S DO THIS THEN--
AND CHOOPIE... NO TROUBLE, YOU HEAR?
'KAY... WE GOT A SIGNAL. IT'S DOWN THERE.
"WHOA! HE'S A BIIIIIG BOGIE...
"...I'LL, UM... TRY TO... UH... OH, WHAT'S IT SAY IN THE BOOK...? UHHH...
" 'MAKE CONTACT WITH TRANSDIMENSIONAL INTERLOPER AND ATTEMPT TO OPEN A NON-THREATENING DIALOGUE'...
" 'KAY...RIGHT... HERE GOES..."

GOOD MORNING? ...UHHHH, WE-ARE-OPERATIVES-OF-THIS-REALITY'S-EXTRA-DIMENSIONAL-MONITORING-AGENCY.
WE-ARE-HERE-TO-INFORM-YOU-THAT-YOU-DO-NOT-HAVE-THE-PROPER-SANCTIONS-TO UHHHH...
VISIT.
OH, THAT'S GOOD... TO-VISIT-THIS-REALM.
IF YOU WOULD, LIKE, PUT DOWN THE, UMM, UNCONSCIOUS HOT CHICK IN THE, UH, VICTORIA'S SECRET? LIKE, PERHAPS WE COULD--

GAHHHH WAHHH!
THE FIRST PIE STORY
TODD AND CRAIG 2K3
COLORS--RICO
OR PERHAPA NOT.
I'M CALLING THAT A 'NO.'
OKAY, MG--

NO, CHOOPIE--
I DIDN'T MEAN
FOR YOU TO--
UH, MOLLY--
I THINK WE'VE GOT MORE IMPORTANT THINGS TO CONSIDER...
...NAMELY, WHERE'D THE BIG GUY GO?
I HIT HIM WITH THE PLASMA-NET, BUT RATHER THAN CONTAIN HIM IN A COCCOON OF ENERGY...IT... IT BAKED HIM! TURNED HIM INTO ALL THIS--
...STEAM...?
NO...
!
NOT STEAM!
IT'S--

AHHH SAHHH GAHHHH WAAAAH!
...HIM.
RELAX, MOLLY.
REMEMBER, YOU'RE A GHOST. YOU'RE ETHEREAL. HE CAN'T HURT YOU. HE CAN'T TOUCH--
AHHH?!
--MG--I COULD FEEL THAT! IT WENT RIGHT THROUGH ME, BUT I COULD FEEL--
WHAT IS THIS GUY...?!
HANG ON, MOL!! I'M COM--
WHUD
--HUNFF!
NAAAAHN!

FUMPP
NOBODY SMACKS MY TEAMMATES 'ROUND WHILE I'M HOLDIN' THIS MESS-YOU-UP GUN...!
LEHH BAHHHG! LEH MEH FOOO!
SKRUNCH
HEY! YOU DOOF! THAT WAS MY FAVORITE GUN!
GAHHHH!
UM, OKAY, YOU GUYS! WE'VE GOT NO IDEA WHAT THIS THING IS!
BUT AS FIELD LEADER, I... I THINK WE SHOULD, LIKE,
RUN!
GOOD PLAN, MOL.
RUN, RUN!
THERE! IN THAT CHURCH!

QUICK, GUYS! GET INSIDE! FIND SOMETHING TO BARRICADE THESE DOORS!
MY LUNCHBOX!!
MG--WHAT... WHAT DO WE DO?! ANY IDEAS?!
I DON'T KNOW, MOL--
HE SHAKES OFF OUR TECH, HE CAN AFFECT YOU... IF WE DON'T FIND SOME WAY TO STOP HIM, WE'RE--
RASSA FRASSIN-- ALL MY PIES! ALL MY JUICEBOXES! I'M GONNA--
WAIT! HE'S COMING!
IT'S GOT US! THERE'S NO WAY--
--OUT! WE'RE TRAPPED!

TODD AND CRAIG'S
THE Perhapanauts
IN
THE MONSTER AND THE PIES!
CORNERED IN A SMALL REMOTE, RURAL CHURCH BY A RELENTLESS, RAMPAGING BRUTE, THE PERHAPANAUTS SUDDENLY FIND THAT THEY ARE--
TRAPPED!!
...LIKE BATS!
RATS.
WHATEVER.
THE HULKING MONSTER LOOMS LARGE IN THE SANCTUARY'S DOORWAY, A MURDEROUS RAGE REFLECTED IN THE BEHEMOTH'S INHUMAN EYES--!
RAAAHHH!
UNTIL ONE OF THOSE EYES HAPPENS TO SPY--
UNHH...?
HEY, LOOK! HE'S STOPPING FOR ONE OF CHOOPIE'S PLAYSWELL FRUIT PIES!
GRRR!? THAT'S MY FRUIT PIE!!
SHUT UP, CHOOPIE. AT LEAST IT CALMED HIM DOWN.
HE'S SMILING AT ME, YOU GUYS!
MMM... GOOOH.
HE MUST REALLY LIKE THE TENDER CRUST AND REAL FRUIT FILLING!
WHO WOULDA BELIEVED PLAYSWELL FRUIT PIES WOULD SAVE THE DAY?!
YOU'LL FEEL SWELL WHEN YOU EAT A PLAYSWELL® FRUIT PIE!
HA HA HA
HA HA
MY FRUIT PIES!

®PLAYSWELL IS A REGISTERED TRADEMARK OF PLAYS WELL WITH OTTERS INC.

UNNNGH!
GOOOH FOOOH PAHHH!
YEAH, THEY ARE GOOD, BUDDY! HAVE ANOTHER!
OUTSIDE, UNSEEN BY ANYONE, THE FIRST PENCIL-THIN RAY OF MORNING SUNLIGHT MAKES IT'S APPEARANCE...
HEY!?
HE'S DRINKIN' MY JUICEBOXES, TOO!! YA BIG GREEDY--
CHOOPIE! SHUT UP!
...AND FINDS IT'S WAY THROUGH THE SANCTUARY'S WINDOW, ONLY TO RESULT IN--
FASSSHHH
UNHGGH!
FIIIE!!
FIIIE!!
FIIIE!!!
OMIGOD!
OMIGOD, WHADDA WE DO?!
EASY, BIG GUY, EASY!
DON'T PANIC! I'M ON IT!
NNNNNNO! NO WAHHH! NO WAHHH!
HO-EEE WAHHH! HO-EEE WAHHH!!!

AAAAHHHHHRRRGGH!! AAEEIII!!!
SSPLORCH
SSSSLIPP
UHHHH NUHHH.
SSHLUCKT
WHOA! LOOK OUT, BUDDY-- YOU'RE GONNA--
THERE IS A MOMENTARY, BLINDING FLASH OF LIGHT...
...AND THEN...
'KAY... WELL, I GUESS THAT SETTLES THAT?
HUH? I WOULDN'T HAVE GUESSED THAT...
WHO'DA THUNK...

...A STINKIN' VAMPIRE!
THAT'S WHAT YOU GET FOR EATING MY FRUIT PIES.
BLOOD-SUCKIN' FREAK.
UHM, CHOOPIE...?
YEAH, TECHNICALLY SPREAKING, CHOOP--AREN'T YOU A BLOOD-SUCKING FREAK?
... YEAH, WELL, WHY DON'T YOU SHUT UP?
YOU SHUT UP.
NO, YOU SHUT UP.
WHY DON'T YOU.
YOU.
YOU.
WHY DO I FEEL LIKE WE'RE FORGETTING SOMETHING?
YOU.
UM... HELLO?
WHU--WHERE--?
AM I ON TV?
END

PIN-UPS

MIKE WIERINGO
GUY DAVIS
RICH WOODALL AND MATT TALBOT
CHRIS BRUNNER
DAVID WILLIAMS
NICK CARDY
KEVIN NOWLAN
DEREK FRIDOLFS
KELLY YATES
JACK LAWRENCE
JONBOY MEYERS
DAVID PETERSEN
SEAN "CHEEKS" GALLOWAY
LUKE ROSS
TED MCKEEVER
ANDY KUHN

mike wieringo
colors by rico

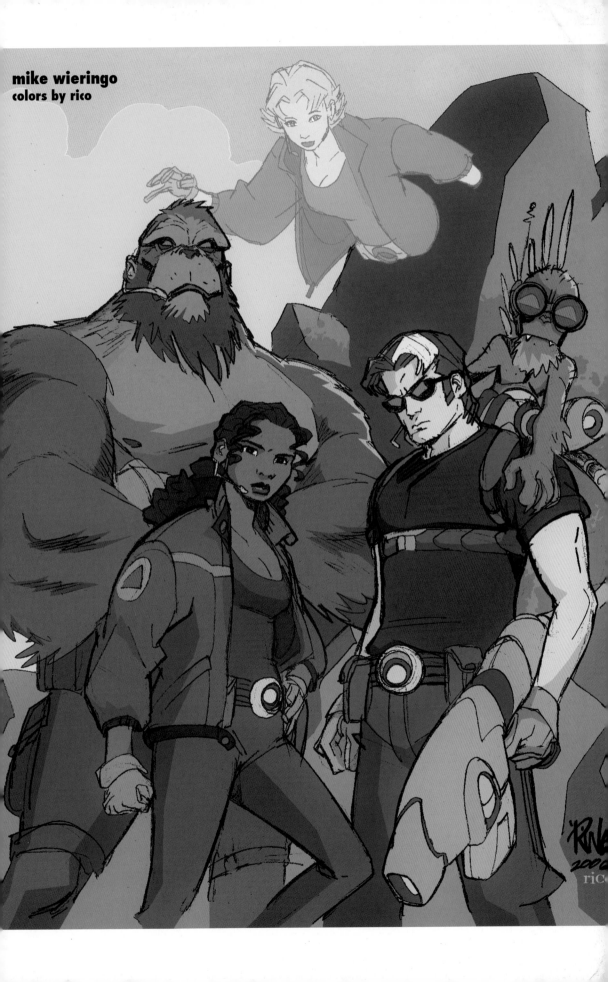

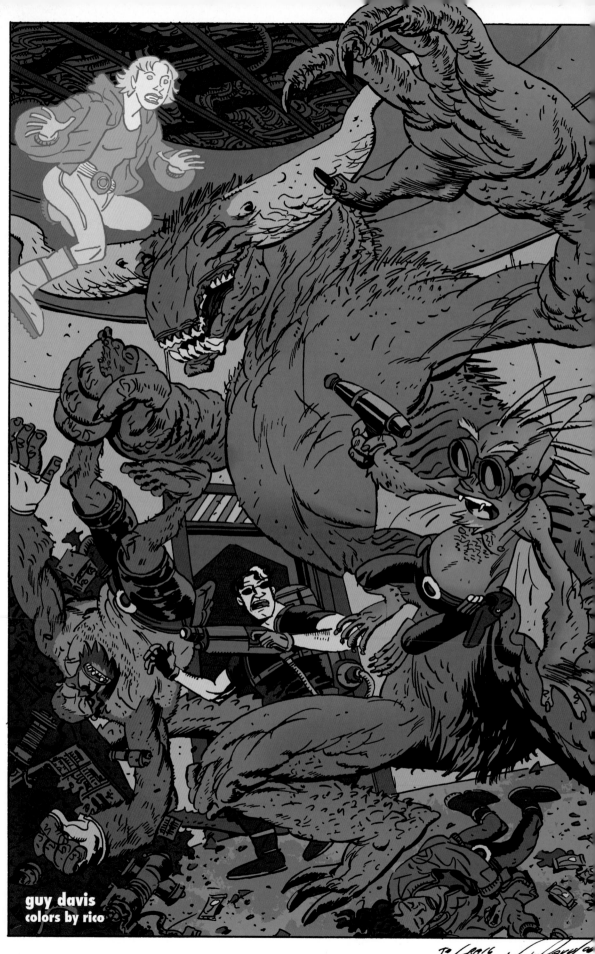

guy davis
colors by rico

TO CRAIG
- CHEERS!

rich woodall and matt talbot
colors by ray dillon

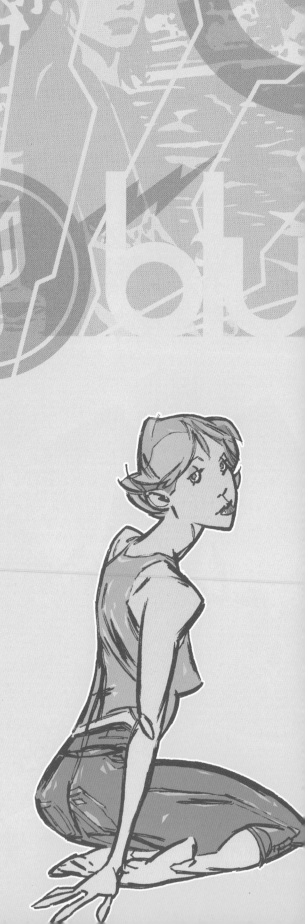

chris brunner
colors by rico

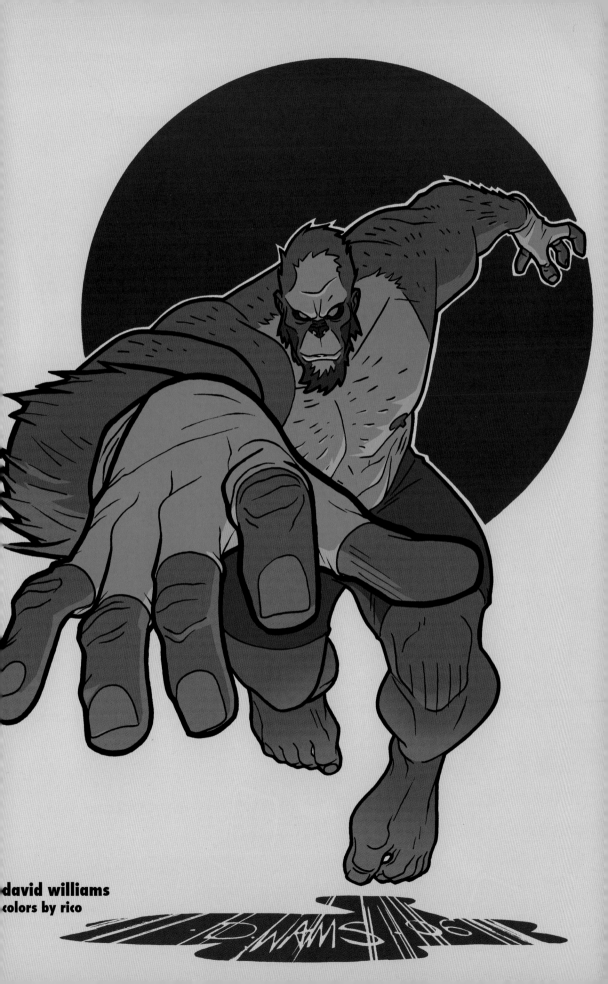

david williams
colors by rico

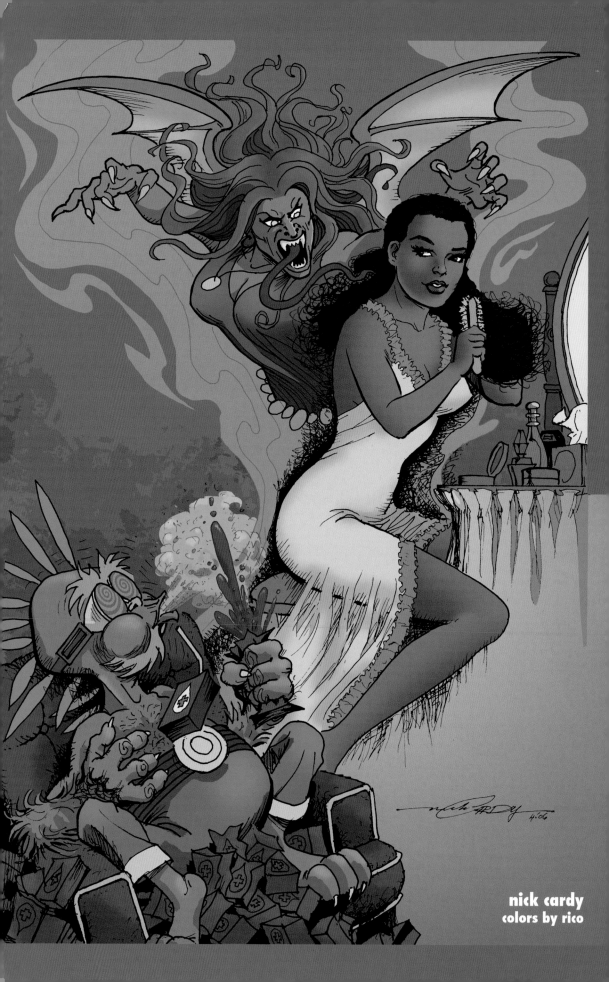

nick cardy
colors by rico

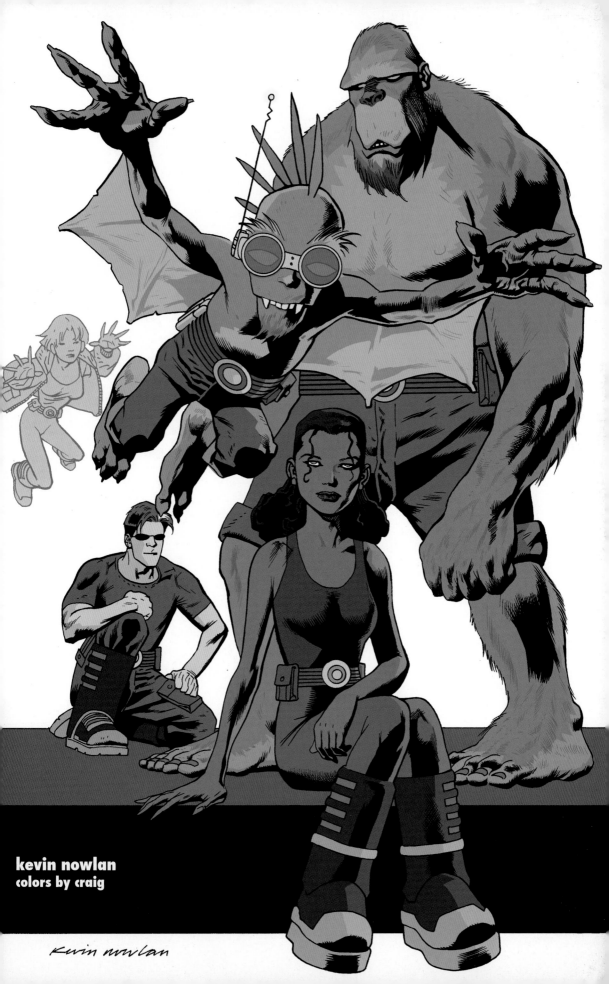

kevin nowlan
colors by craig

kevin nowlan

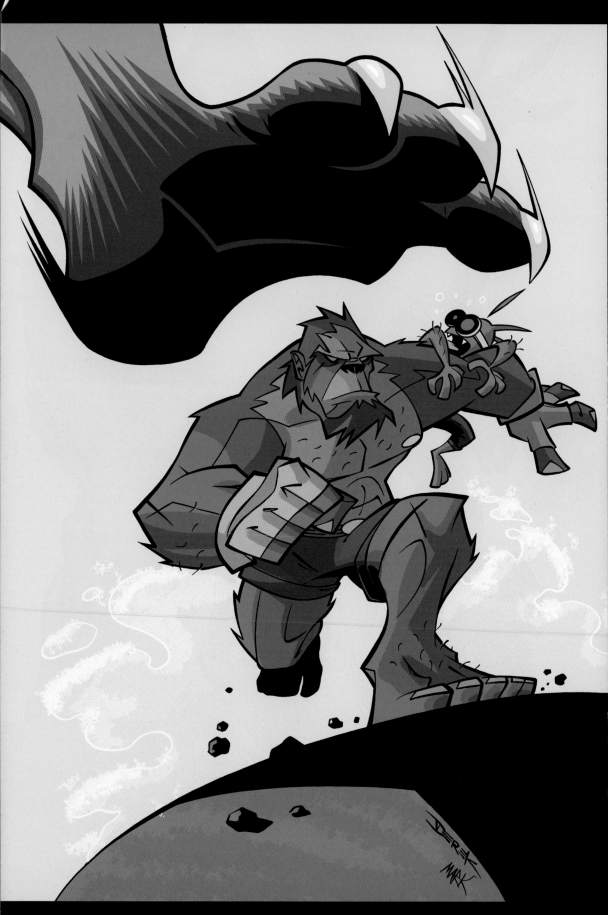

derek fridolfs
colors by mark englert

elly yates

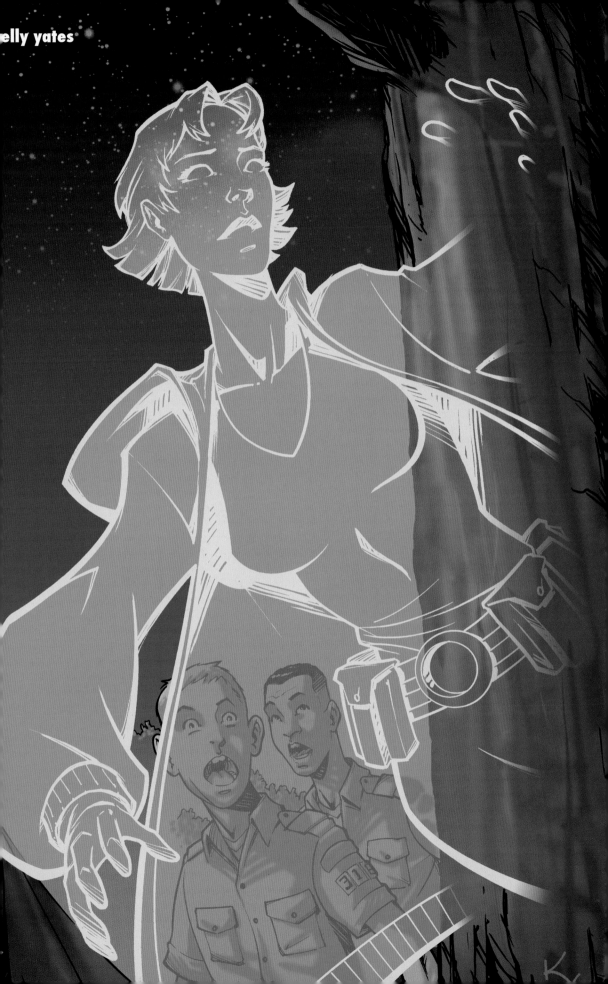

jonboy meyers
colors by scott kester

GENIUS AT WORK
GOATS weekly
craig draws comics.
TODD AND CRAIG'S
THE Perhapanaut
JONBOY! '07
12:21

david petersen

sean "cheeks" galloway

luke ross

EL VARGINHA
LROSS

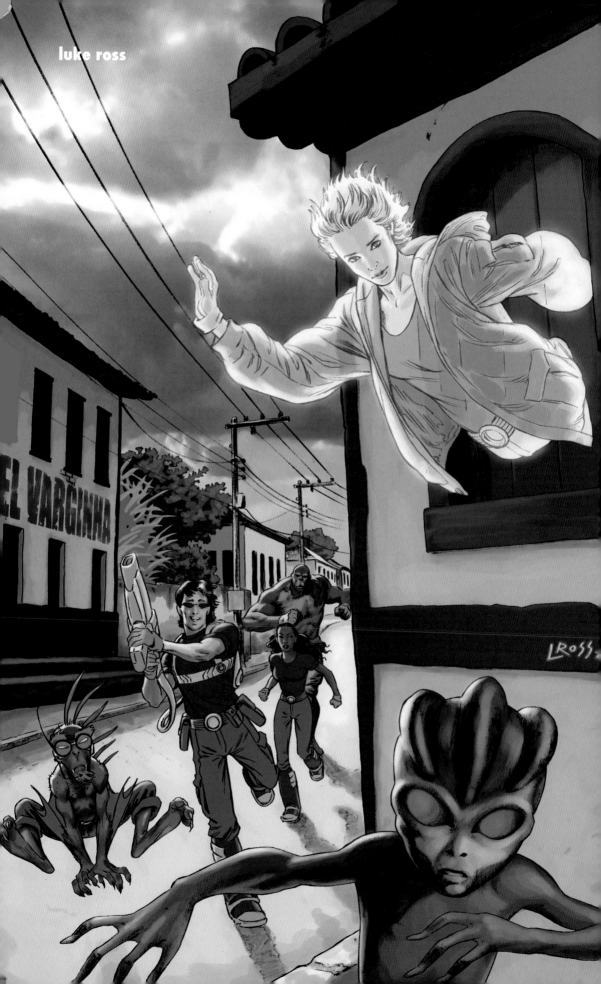

ted mckeever

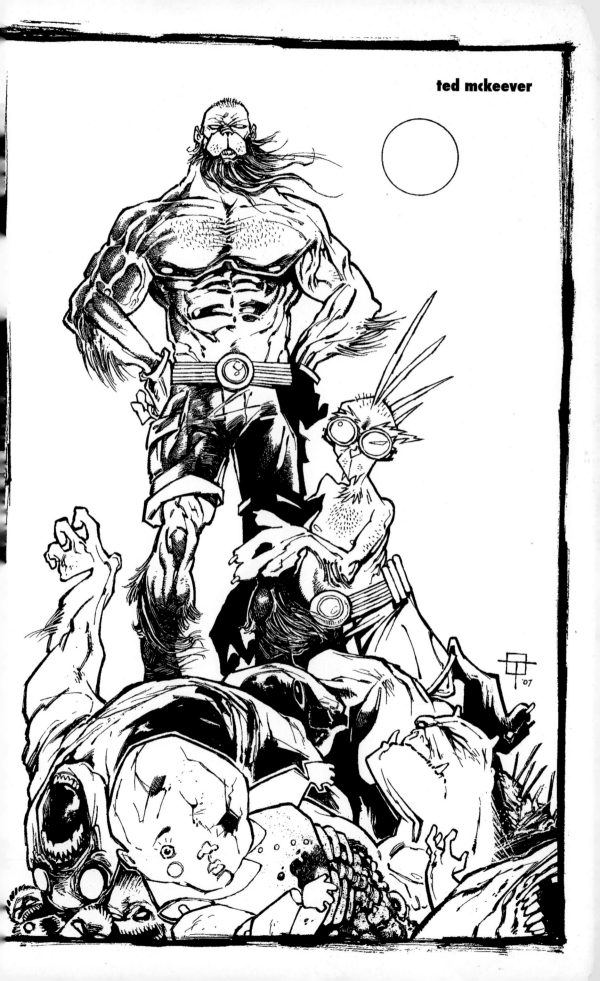

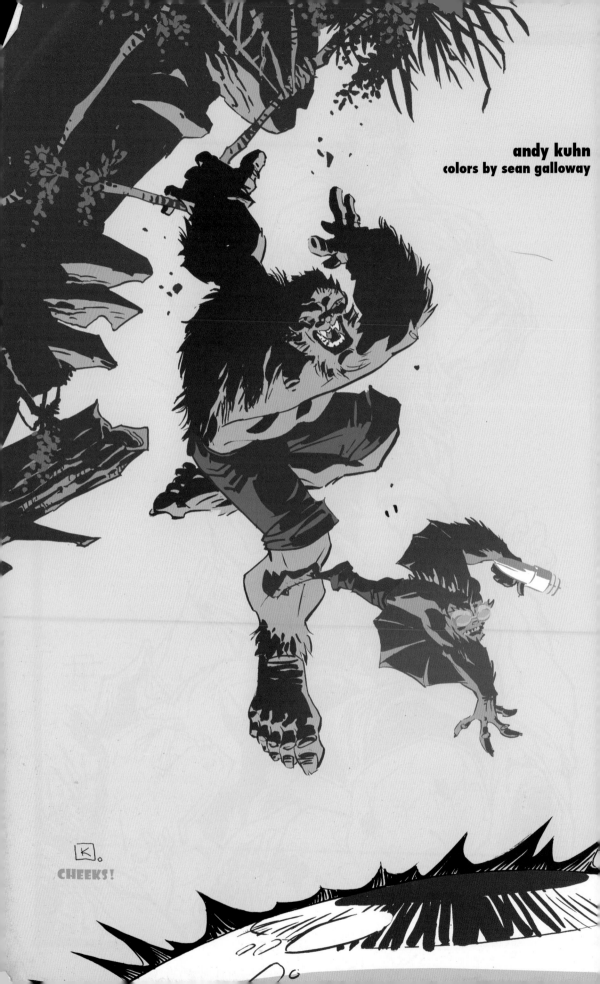

andy kuhn
colors by sean galloway